DESIGNING
WITH
COLLECTIBLES

SIMON &
SCHUSTER

CANDACE ORD MANROE

DESIGNING WITH COLLECTIBLES

SIMON & SCHUSTER

London   Sydney   New York   Tokyo   Toronto   Singapore

A FRIEDMAN GROUP BOOK

SIMON & SCHUSTER
Simon & Schuster Building
Rockefeller Center
1230 Avenue of the Americas
New York, NY 10020

DESIGNING WITH COLLECTIBLES
was prepared and produced by
Michael Friedman Publishing Group, Inc.
15 West 26th Street
New York, NY 10010

Editor: Sharyn Rosart
Art Director: Jeff Batzli
Designer: Ed Noriega
Photography Editor: Daniella Jo Nilva
Typeset by Classic Type, Inc.
Printed and bound in Hong Kong by Leefung-Asco Printers Ltd.

10 9 8 7 6 5 4 3 2 1

Library of Congress Cataloging in Publication Data

Manroe, Candace Ord, 1954–
       Designing with collectibles/Candace Ord Manroe.
              p.   cm.
       Includes index.
       ISBN 0-671-76103-X
       1. Collectibles in interior decoration.   1. Title.
NK2115.5.C58M36   1992
747' g—dc20   92-30120
                                     CIP
ISBN: 0-671-76103-X

The publishers would like to thank all the collectors who so kindly allowed us
to photograph their treasures.

ACKNOWLEDGEMENTS

Special thanks to Michael Graham for sharing his design expertise and to the staff at the Friedman Group for putting this project together.

DEDICATION

To my parents, whose love of collecting has continued to the next generation and to Meagan and Drew, who will continue the tradition.

TABLE OF CONTENTS

INTRODUCTION

CONFESSIONS OF A CONGENITAL COLLECTOR

Growing up in a family of pack rats that stood several generations deep, I chose the path of rebellion over conformity. Early on, I vowed that my personal living space would not be cluttered with bric-a-brac—a lot of "old stuff" that caught dust and cobwebs, and not my heart. My tabletops, shelves, cabinets, and countertops would be swept clean of collectibles, not entombed in memorabilia of the past.

I knew exactly how I wanted my rooms to look: One piece of art, arresting and powerful, would fully engage the senses in any given space, negating the need for more. My dream home would be a paragon of impeccable, tempered taste, pure and simple.

A few decades later, I've yet to see this minimalistic home. In other words, I've yet to see myself divested of the collectibles and the collecting instinct that are my birthright.

My feeble efforts at paring down inevitably have wound up with me falling over piles of—what else?—stuff: collec-

tions of Southwestern art, English pottery, old family photographs, and books; those things I alternately lament as excess baggage and cling to as my travel mates for life.

Anyone who collects, I believe, can sympathize with my frustration at times over who's in charge here: them or me?

Collections, as the name makes clear, by nature tend to accrue. The challenge lies in learning how to manage our collections: how and where to display them in a manner that blends harmoniously with the remainder of the home; how to ensure that their quiet but steady proliferation doesn't one day prove disastrous, unduly dominating our carefully designed spaces. (See chapter 4).

Once this threat is conquered, living with collectibles can supply a deeply satisfying feeling that's simply unattainable in an austerely decorated home.

Chrome domestic products from the art deco period, including pieces as utilitarian as an electric toaster, create a stylish effect when grouped as a collection.

CHAPTER ONE

WHY COLLECT?

What is it about collectibles, anyway, that fosters such a feeling of fulfillment for the owners—that serves as fodder for the soul? How is it that a number of inanimate objects can spark real animation in their collector—and in their home?

The prevailing reason for collecting, both in terms of number and importance, is passion. People collect the things they love. The primary impetus for collecting, then, is emotional. Stirred by the heart, people collect the things they love based on two different criteria—that is, from two different approaches: intrinsic and associative. Collecting that is not a matter of the emotions usually can be identified as either decorative or investment collecting.

Previous page: This collection of pails, dating from 1910 to 1950, serves as a colorful, one-of-a-kind focal point when arrayed on one shelf of a bookcase otherwise filled with the expected volumes.

Intrinsic Collecting

The first approach we will call intrinsic, for it describes a kind of emotional collecting that is centered entirely on the objects' intrinsic appeal. This approach primarily is an expression of aesthetic sensibilities, with objects collected entirely because of their physical merits.

Take a collection of elliptical-shaped, blue-glaze vases, for example. The distinct form, color, and texture are what appeal to the collector. Outside the realm of beauty, sentiment is not an issue here. It makes no difference if the next vase in the collection is found at an out-of-town auction during a memorable weekend of romance, or on the third floor of a department store during a quick lunch-hour shopping spree.

What matters is the object itself, not what it represents. With intrinsic collecting, the object's meaning is self-contained, not contingent on any associations.

The collectible vase may be one of a slightly larger or smaller size than others in the group, and it may have a ridged texture unlike anything else in the collection; therefore, this vase becomes extremely desirable in the eyes of the collector.

On the other hand, an exquisite vase featuring fine craftsmanship may be passed up, to the perplexity of the collector's companions. What renders the second vase unacceptable is not its lack of beauty, but its absence of those specific qualities—precisely the right shape and color—that spark passion for the highly discerning collector.

Opposite page: Throwaway items from the past such as old tobacco tins possess interesting shapes, colors, and a note of nostalgia that makes them popular among collectors.

Associative Collecting

The second approach to collecting is best termed associative. Baseball card collectors, as a rule, are associative collectors. They associate the collected object with something else —in this case, baseball—which is their real passion. These collectors search out cards not for their intrinsic appeal but for their association with the game—for what the cards represent about the sport that is the collector's true love.

A nine-year-old friend of mine, Zachary Biggs, has been a baseball collector for five years, initially motivated by his father's—then his own—love of the game. Though it was the game and the cards per se that got him hooked, the resulting collection is now a point of pride in its own right for Zachary: It is amazingly thorough and valuable, and he knows it.

Whatever their chosen field of collectibles, associative collectors are alike in being one step removed from their true field of interest, of which the collectible is only a symbol.

New York City actress S. Epatha Merkerson, a Tony nominee for her lead in *The Piano Lesson,* is an associative collector; New York City antiques dealer Alan Moss is an intrinsic collector. Their approaches to collecting are clearly different.

Epatha collects black memorabilia, especially sheet music. These collectibles help put her, as a black woman in the entertainment industry, in touch with her past—in touch with the struggles and the stereotypes that confronted, and were overcome by, her black predecessors in show business.

"My original reason for collecting was anger. I knew black memorabilia was in vogue again. White people made money on it the first time, and I knew today's white collectors would make money on it again, so I decided to buy everything I could," she explained.

But somewhere along the way, her motivation changed. Epatha started seeing aspects of her own story in the black memorabilia—the history of prejudice toward all members of her race. "I started seeing collecting as a way of preserving my history," she said.

© Michael Grand

Opposite page, top: This collection of Star Trek memorabilia is an example of associative collecting: The Star Trek shows, more than the intrinsic qualities of the pieces, are the real source of meaning.
Opposite page, bottom: Love of the game of baseball sponsored this collection of memorabilia.
Above: Similarly, this still-life of flight jacket, goggles, and related objects was inspired by a passion for flying.

An Aunt Jemima cookie jar does not appeal to Epatha through its intrinsic qualities—it was mass-produced from cheap materials and exudes no special beauty. To the contrary, far from being inherently charming, the Aunt Jemima and many other pieces of African-American memorabilia are revolting in their gross stereotyping of an entire race.

But because of what even the most undignified characterization in black memorabilia represents—a sad chapter of overt racism in history—they have value to Epatha. She never wants to forget the struggles of African-Americans—the determination and courage it took to live in a society in which insidious slurs, defamation, and hatred were all too common. Items that are pure kitsch—ashtrays depicting naked black children eating watermelons, for example—would interest Epatha as collectibles because of their associative appeal.

Among Epatha's collectibles is a piece of sheet music, "Campmeetin' Time," illustrated with a black southern preacher in the act of stealing a chicken; another, "Dan, Dan, Danuel," bears the description, "a crazy coon concoction." These items are especially prized by Epatha, for they reveal a stereotype that was a hard, humiliating fact of life regularly faced by her precursors in show business. Because of their specific association to her own story as an actress, the musical items are of greater value to Epatha than other forms of memorabilia in her collection. And should a piece of sheet music happen to be a gift from a friend, its meaning is further enhanced, for it carries yet another association for her.

Right and opposite page, top: Aunt Jemimas and other black memorabilia provide an erstwhile, folksy feeling in this room. To many black collectors, the stereotype pieces represent a painful but important chapter of black history and are therefore appreciated for their associative, not inherent, function.

Alan Moss, on the other hand, is also an emotional collector, but one whose collecting is not motivated by associations. He has one of the world's best and most extensive collections of Puerto Rican *santos*—the small, painted wood carvings of saints. These naive carvings have been revered for centuries by Puerto Rico's pious Catholics as tangible representations of the saints to whom believers turned to mediate their prayers and petitions. But religious association is not among Alan's reasons for collecting *santos*. And although some members of his family have lived in Puerto Rico, ethnic identity is not a motivation for his collecting, either.

Alan's approach to collecting *santos* is intrinsic. He appreciates *santos* entirely as folk art—for the aesthetic appeal inherent in their primitive, folksy charm. To be deemed worthy of his collection, each *santo* must have an unusual, aesthetically pleasing appearance or in some way fill a void not met by the other *santos* he owns. A *santo* hailing from the part of the island where his family lived, then, would not necessarily have more appeal than any other piece, for Alan's approach to collecting is intrinsic, not associative.

Nor does it matter much if the *santo* is a gift or the result of tricky negotiating that starts with a picker (a person whose job is locating antiques and collectibles for dealers and individual collectors). The end result is what counts, not any sentimentality along the way.

Although the two types of passionate collecting constitute the most prevalent and important reasons for collecting, at least two additional motivations must be addressed. These reasons for collecting are decoration and investment.

Left: Native-American kachinas, baskets, and storyteller pottery figures.

Above: This collection of carefully worked silver boxes lends an elegant and formal feeling to a room. *Opposite page:* A group of vintage pillows in lush, fringed fabrics is a key decorative element in this space.

Decorative Collecting

Collecting for the sole purpose of decorating a home—of filling space—typically begins with shallow roots that grow deeper as the collection itself grows. For as a collection is amassed, with it usually comes the increased knowledge and serious interest of the collector.

Who hasn't, at some point in decorating a home, apartment, or even a college dorm room, spied a wall, corner, or cabinet that simply didn't accommodate existing furnishings; that needed a little help to blend with an overall design? It is under these casual circumstances that truly good collections sometimes are born.

Consider this case in point: "I bought a circa-1820 corner cupboard for its wonderful original blue paint, but I'm not a country design person," one woman complained. "Now that I have it, what do I put in it?"

This homeowner's existing collection of china and contemporary pottery already was in place in another part of the home. For her, the obvious solution to the problem of putting the antique corner cupboard to good service was to begin a new collection of objects that would appropriately fill it.

The homeowner finally decided on antique pewter as her new field of collecting. "I like the patina of old pewter, and I like the variety of shapes made from pewter," she said.

At first, she began purchasing any pewter that pleased her, without considering the vintage. But as the budding collection went full bloom, she became more discerning. Before long, the focus of the pewter collection had narrowed; within its range were only American pewter pieces made around the same era as the corner cupboard itself.

When first-time guests to the home comment on the pewter, the owner honestly admits its superficial origins as a decorative device—as a space filler. But then she enthusiastically launches into conversation about the individual pieces in the collection—their genesis, function, special distinctions, and charm.

What started simply as decorative collecting, somewhere along the way became passionate—specifically, passionate intrinsic collecting.

Above: A collection of antique pewter displayed in a corner cupboard.

At the opposite end of the spectrum from the pewter collector is another, less common type of decorative collector: the type who never warms to a collection, who never takes a real interest, who could just as easily have entirely different genres of collectibles taking up space, for as little difference as it would make. This apathetic person is a collector only in the sense of laying down the cash to pay for the collectibles.

Usually, this person is working with a designer and has, in fact, turned over all responsibility for the home's appearance and character to this third party. The carte blanche given the designer, in fact, is an almost sure sign of a commensurate amount of disinterest on the part of the homeowner. All that matters to this collector is that the house be done "right"—that it have the right look and be filled with the right objects. If this entails collections, fine, so long as they have a pedigree that announces a level of prestige in keeping with that of the collector's self-image, or a style that's in general accordance with the homeowner's taste.

Investment Collecting

The last category of collecting—investment—can be either fiery with emotion or coolly dispassionate. The point in investment collecting is that any item purchased for a collection must satisfy one chief criterion: It must have documented value and also be considered likely to appreciate in value over time.

A majority of the world's greatest collectors do not overlook investment when making their selections. Monetary value, however, usually is not the only—or the most important—reason for their collecting, although it may be a deciding factor.

One collector of nineteenth-century folk art paintings, for instance, did not initiate his collection out of the conviction that one day he would get a good return on his dollar. His collection got its start straight from his heart, not his bank statement. He saw one painting that deeply moved him, and he bought it. He was so pleased with the initial pur-

Above left: Fine art is generally chosen not only for its visual and emotional impact, but also according to investment value, which is based on rarity and condition. *Above right:* These valuable pre-Columbian figures include a pregnant woman, right, and a mother and her twin children seated on a swing, left. *Left:* Among these ancient artifacts is a head from Angkor Wat. For such precious collections, customized display units are generally best.

chase that it inspired others; the next thing he knew, he was a collector.

These days, when he buys folk art canvases, he has enough knowledge and intuition to know what's really good—and he buys only good art. He thinks about a piece's value as an investment, then, but still buys only art that truly inspires him. The idea of purchasing a painting he doesn't like simply because it is the work of a well-known folk artist would be unthinkable.

Consummate collectors stress value—buying the best quality you can possibly afford—with the attendant hope that the purchase will retain its value or escalate in worth. But should a piece be riveting yet clearly not a good investment, an overwhelming majority of serious collectors would advise buying it anyway. Besides, once a collector's eye has been cultivated, it is unlikely that he or she would be drawn to a piece that is not of investment quality.

So collecting for investment, then, doesn't necessarily have pejorative connotations or imply any calculating, mercenary mentality. Instead, it can point to quite the opposite: to the collector's advanced level of seriousness and discernment.

Above: These Russian lacquer boxes form a valuable and attractive collection. *Opposite page:* A graceful arrangement of nineteenth-century picture frames, crystal, magnifying glasses and other objects perfectly complements this Victorian interior.

CHAPTER TWO

BUILDING COLLECTIONS ON A FIRM FOUNDATION

Previous page: This collection
of old radios, arranged by size
and shape, makes an arresting
display. *Right:* Collecting the
porcelain figures beautifully
displayed in the niches of this
secretary requires a finely
tuned eye able to discern the
subtle differences that distinguish good pieces from inferior or even reproduction
items.

Early on as a design writer, after I had written several pieces on homes that included collections of Staffordshire dogs in their design, I knew the time had come to break my own rule; it was time to venture into the world of collecting.

Staffordshire dogs—specifically, the King Charles spaniels glazed a russet hue on white—appealed to me. As a dog person, I naturally felt an affection for these objects.

In addition, I admired the plebeian roots of Staffordshire figures. Throughout the nineteenth century, and beginning even earlier, pottery from England's clay-rich Staffordshire district had served as the poor man's porcelain, allowing working-class people who couldn't afford real porcelain to adorn their homes, anyway. Although the actual design of Staffordshire dogs wasn't one that I necessarily found extraordinary, or even very good, the emotional messages these spaniels were signaling gave me reason enough to want to collect.

Having developed an interest in a specific collectible, the next step was getting started—how to go about turning that interest into a tangible collection. But before I explain how that process occurred, be forewarned: My entree into collecting is not standard—not a method any seasoned collector would advise. I share my story to make this point: Even collecting rules have their exceptions. The lesson from my experience is that being a rigid rule stickler can mean lost opportunity in launching a collection.

The story begins with competitive airfares resulting in an unexpected trip to England. Knowing that the Staffordshire dogs I was interested in collecting hailed from there, I ideally would have researched my subject beforehand and made my trip armed with information on quality, price, and age. But the spur-of-the-moment circumstances of the trip did not afford me that luxury. If I found Staffordshire dogs in England, I would have to make a decision based on pure intuition and heart. Realizing this even before boarding the plane, I decided not to search for Staffordshire; to wait until I could buy wisely, from a more informed position.

But just as I hadn't expected to be going to England in the first place, neither had I anticipated a fierce thunderstorm running me out of the narrow, cobblestoned streets of Canterbury into the first open building for shelter.

Here, amidst a dreary array of dinged pots and pans, chipped china, and miscellaneous unmatched silver-plate flatware, I spotted a pair of white-and-russet pottery dogs in the corner of a booth.

Sure enough, I had found a matched pair of Staffordshire spaniels. The coloration was right (Staffordshire dogs are also glazed with other colors), and the size was similar to others I had seen—which meant, to an insecure potential collector, comfort in number. Picking up the dogs, I was fairly certain that the tiny crack lines (not breaks) and patina were authentic signs of age; the modeling of the design itself was clean and distinct.

I knew nothing about the going price of a pair of dogs, but when the dealer negotiated, I bought.

Pleased with my purchase, I scanned the woman's booth once more before leaving, taking in those items I hadn't seen at all after spying my dogs. To my surprise, there sat another Staffordshire dog—this one with the same coloration as the pair I had just bought, but much smaller in size, and on a plinth, as opposed to freestanding. The small dog had a bad crack, the result of a break, that had been poorly repaired, and it had the most unusual eyes I had ever seen on a Staffordshire dog.

Although I was charmed by the dog, I had no confidence in my judgment, as is often the case with neophyte collectors. My limited knowledge about collecting in general told me that damage reduces value—and that a shoddy repair job brings it down even more.

I passed on the charming little dog.

When I returned to the United States, I promptly visited an antiques shop specializing in English pieces, especially Staffordshire pottery. The good news I learned from the dealer was that the pair of dogs I had bought in Canterbury were of good quality—and were selling for almost five times the amount that I had paid.

The bad news was that the dog I did not buy was indeed rare, and, despite its damage, would have been a good addition to a collection. But I didn't need anyone telling me that. From the moment I boarded a train back to London, I had longed for the puzzling pottery dog with the enigmatic eyes.

Fifteen years later, I continue to regret not having made that purchase. I've never seen another Staffordshire dog like the one I passed up.

Go With Your Heart

Both the good and bad sides of this collecting tale emphasize one important principle of collecting: Go with your heart.

Whenever a collectible speaks to you, evoking strong emotion, follow your instincts. The special impact this collectible has on you will ensure years of enjoyment through ownership. To pass it up is a sure ticket to regret.

Don't confuse simple attraction with this stronger tug at the heartstrings, however. Many collectibles can and will catch your eye. Far fewer induce an intense, almost visceral response. Know the difference. When the attraction is deep, act on it.

Right: The more unlikely the collection, the more interesting it will be. There's nothing priceless about this collection of brushes, for example, but the individual objects, when grouped together in a balanced arrangement with varying heights and shapes, is packed with visual power and intrigue. *Opposite page:* This grouping of Memoryware objects gives these individually unremarkable pieces a context in which their unique appeal can be appreciated.

Ignore Convention

If your heart is moved by a collectible, don't allow convention to stand in your way. Items do not have to be in vogue to merit collecting. This generation's first collectors of Fiestaware were ahead of their time: They bought the dinnerware because they liked it, despite the fact that no one else thought the pottery was good for much other than the trash heap or a garage sale. These days, Fiestaware has grown enormously in popularity—to the delight of those first collectors who dared venture outside the mainstream.

Educate Yourself

My Staffordshire dog experience underscores an additional principle of collecting: If at all possible, educate yourself thoroughly in your field of interest before beginning to collect.

Had I had more exposure to Staffordshire dogs, I would have known that the small plinth-base dog I was admiring in Canterbury was highly unusual and was cast from an old mold whose use had never been widespread. My doubts about its value, despite its damage and poor restoration, would have been quelled. Education would have equipped me with the confidence I needed to make the purchase. Researching my genre of collectibles beforehand would have spared me fifteen years of futile search for a similar dog.

Research obviously entails reading in your subject of interest. For a new collector, the best starting point is the public library. Here you will have available a wider offering of reference materials than you probably will be able to find at any generic bookstore.

Even if you are fortunate enough to have a specialty bookstore in your area, a visit to the library first still has its advantages. At the library, you can check out as many books as you want on the subject, with no financial commitment.

Once you've ascertained which of the library books are worth keeping, head for the retail bookstore to pick up copies or place an order. Even if none of the library books are volumes you feel are indispensable, they will at least give you background in the field, which will enable you to make wiser selections at the bookstore.

Libraries also keep older, even out-of-print publications on the shelf, unlike most bookstores, which tend to promote newer material. Unless your collecting field is brand new, some of the best—the truly seminal—writings on the subject may be among the oldest.

After reading literally everything you can put your hands on in book form and purchasing those books that you deem will be continually most helpful throughout your period of collecting, make another visit to the library.

Already you've mastered the fundamentals of your field, steeping yourself in its facts and forms. Now it's time to get current—to acquaint yourself with what's happening today in your field of collectibles. On this visit to the library, then, consult periodicals. Ask the librarian for assistance if you're unfamiliar with how to use the Reader's Guide, your key to locating your subject in magazine articles.

Articles in periodicals will give you current price information that dates too quickly in books. Magazines will also inform you as to where the major activity in your field is occurring—where the important auctions and dealers are located. They will also clue you in on who are the most important collectors—your competition. Periodicals are also valuable for providing you with the latest in research, which has not yet been compiled in book form.

When researching periodicals, it is not necessary to rely solely on memory. Don't hesitate to make photocopies of articles that strike you as particularly informative. As with books, determine which magazines devote the most attention to your field, then get subscriptions of your own. This way, you will be able to easily, painlessly stay abreast of happenings with your collectibles, without further research missions to the periodicals section of your library.

To truly become educated in a field of collecting, however, you need more than the printed word. There is no substitute for hands-on exposure to your collectibles. From your research, you will have learned which museums and/or galleries offer exhibitions of your subject. Visit them.

Study the museum pieces carefully, for these are the stellar examples that set the standard in your field. Look at construction, craftsmanship, design, color, scale—all the variables that determine quality for your collectible. Note

Opposite page: A vast knowledge of musical instruments enabled this collector to amass this stunning collection of instruments from all over the world.

the differences in style among individual makers or manufacturers. And don't be afraid to form your own opinion, even if it means rejecting a work represented in the museum's collection.

The advantage in viewing a museum's collection is the assured caliber of the pieces. The disadvantage is the inability to touch—to freely turn the collectibles over in your hand and examine all parts. So to augment the knowledge you've gleaned from museums and galleries, it's important to visit antiques shops or retail businesses that carry your collectible.

Under the owner's supervision, you will be able to get a tactile sense of the collectibles and carefully investigate how they are made. Also, talking with a dealer gives you the opportunity to obtain answers to any questions you might have formulated as a result of your earlier visits to libraries and museums. Once a reputable dealer becomes aware of the seriousness of your interest, he or she usually will be happy to share expertise. In the process, you will become a better collector—and a better customer for the dealer.

Cultivating these kinds of relationships early on will pay off later, as your collection becomes more and more refined and specific pieces of interest to you become fewer and fewer. The dealer with a comprehensive understanding of your col-

lecting interests can stay alert for any suitable pieces that might come on the market.

In addition to firsthand contact with collectibles through museums, galleries, and dealers, attend auctions whenever possible. This is where many of the truly great items—museum quality, but still privately owned—are sold. Not only will you get a rare chance to see these collectibles, you will be able to get a feel for their market value in a way that is impossible when you work with a dealer. (You know the dealer's price, but not whether the public agrees with it. At an auction, you immediately learn how much other collectors are willing to spend.)

Plus, better auctions offer catalogs that are good reference materials—indeed, with their four-color photographs, some catalogs are almost works of art themselves.

Having developed expertise in your field of interest through primary and secondary research (people/products, and books/magazines), and knowing that it's best to go with your heart, you are well on your way to being ready to begin a collection that will give you years of pleasure. These two basic principles constitute the core of successful collecting. If you're clever enough to master them, becoming a powerhouse of knowledge while still staying sensitive to matters of the heart regarding your field of collecting, com-

Thanks mostly to the influence of Andy Warhol's personal collection, cookie jars rose to prominence as a hot collectible—one that need not be relegated to the kitchen.

© Alex McLean

Left: These bells, gongs, and triangles have been fitted into specially cut niches, allowing each one to be played. The grouping of similar instruments from different cultures makes for visual harmony as well.

mon sense certainly will carry you through the specific challenges you may face in building your collection. Still, there are a few other guideposts that may be helpful as you prepare to collect.

Buy for Quality

First, buy the best quality you can possibly afford. In other words, if as a new collector you have budgeted, say, $500 for a purchase, spend the entire amount or the bulk of it on a single piece or a couple of pieces that will give you the highest possible quality. Don't fall into the trap of quantity, buying several items simply because it is possible to do so and seems like a greater value. Although you understandably will be eager to amass a sizable collection as soon as possible, true collecting is not an overnight activity. It is a slow, ongoing process that, really, is never "finished." One of its rewards, in fact, is the deep meaning that comes as a result of careful, plodding acquisition over time. Remember, too, that no collectible you purchase is money lost. You can turn around and sell virtually any item.

Consider Bargain Buys, Too

Although a general rule of collecting is to buy the best quality you can afford, this in no way implies that inexpensive collectibles should be ignored. Not only is that snobbery, it's stupidity. If a fifty-cent item at a flea market appeals, buy it. The

Right: Developing a rapport with an antique dealer is an important step in collecting. Whether your interest is rocking horses, wooden crates, or antique sleds, a reliable dealer can give you honest information and keep an eye open for pieces that might interest you. *Opposite page:* Flea markets are excellent sources of vintage pieces like these lunch boxes, which, in addition to their sentimental worth, are becoming increasingly valuable as collectibles.

interest a collection wields has little to do with its price tag. Giveaway novelty items can often add more vigor to a room than expensive pieces. Tarnished oil cans you can pick up for pennies at a garage sale, for instance, have interesting shapes that can make the statement of sculpture.

Upgrade

Often, young collectors will find that, as their incomes rise, so do their capacities to invest in higher-quality collectibles. There is no crime in trading in a beloved collectible that has served you well for one of a higher pedigree that can serve you even better. Upgrading is an understood byword in collecting circles.

CHAPTER THREE

DECIDING WHAT TO COLLECT

As an interior design editor, I periodically field telephone inquiries from toll-free callers having trouble decorating their homes. The questions are diverse, but nearly all of them share one common theme: insecurity.

Each of the callers I speak with are terrified of making a decorating mistake in their homes. What they want, more than anything, is permission—permission to go ahead and implement the decorating ideas they already have.

The caller who helped me identify this common problem was a woman inquiring about remodeling her basement. We chatted for a while, discussing how the space would function for her family, and then she asked me: "What colors should I use?" I paused, not sure I had heard correctly. Then I gave her the only answer possible: "Why, the colors you like."

The problem that plagued this caller, and scores of others like her, really had nothing to do with color. It had to do with a deep insecurity that prevented her from being in touch with her own personal preferences. This insecurity debilitated her, preventing her from taking any decisive action without first clearing it, getting the go-ahead from another source whose opinion she felt was more valid than her own.

The insecurity homeowners feel when it's time to design their homes' interiors is the same phenomenon that is at work with many potential collectors. I am convinced that many people who would delight in collecting never take the plunge, unable to decide what to collect because of paralyzing insecurity.

© Tim Lee

Previous page: When the group falls under the unifying theme of country Americana, a collection can be as open-ended as a plethora of discrete objects from game boards to birdhouses and even to old doorstops.

Above: The best collections are those that are the most personal. Antique china dolls banked in a high chair aren't for everyone, but they make a strong statement about their collector. ***Opposite page:*** Seek the unusual collectible if your goal is to establish a mood of sheer fun. This collection of old metal party horns, arranged in front of the horn poster, creates a nostalgic and festive mood. ***Below:*** Ephemera such as travel postcards, many of which are highly colorful and richly illustrated, add an offbeat splash of character to a room.

© Jennifer Lévy

© Christopher C. Bain

Some mild degree of uncertainty is understandable. When people embark on a new pursuit such as collecting, they want to make sure their investment of time and money will be personally rewarding. But a large number of potential collectors also want to know that these investments will be generally approved—that is, admired by the eyes of the world.

After a lifetime of looking outside themselves for validation, many people have managed to get so out of touch with themselves that they really do not know any longer what they like or dislike. They can't distinguish the difference. They need a direction and a seal of approval for everything, including something that smacks of the personal: a collectible.

This is an unfortunate reality, for nothing stamps a home with an imprint of its owner's personality as much as its collections. Furniture can be perfect, architecture outstanding, but it is the details—the collectibles that accessorize a space—that animate a home with the warmth and vitality of its owner.

Collect the Things You Love

The first commonsense rule in deciding what to collect, then, is to collect the things you love. If a certain type of object gives you pleasure or excites your imagination, you cannot go wrong.

Right: This airy loft reverberates with the sounds of the owner's large collection of musical instruments. The magnificent harps lend a sculptural touch, while wind chimes continue the theme.

© Alex McLean

Above: Drifting among the
hanging plants, the wind
chimes are all attached by a
thin length of wire. With one
tug, their airy tones echo
through the room—a music
lover's paradise.

DECIDING WHAT TO COLLECT

Collect a Style Appropriate for Your Home

Start, perhaps, with the overall style of your home: is it high-tech contemporary, formal traditional, or casual country? If a collectible seems grossly at odds with your home's style, then dismiss it from consideration. On the other hand, assuming that you're comfortable with your home's decorating style, then logic says you will be equally pleased with a collection that blends with that overall decor. Collect a style that meshes with the style of your home.

If your home is minimalistic contemporary, with crisp white walls and European furniture, a collection of contemporary art might work well for you. Or if you want more eclecticism, more funk and more fun, perhaps outsider art is more in keeping with your goals.

Collecting items that suit the decor of your home does not necessarily mean you have to collect precisely the same style as that of your interior design. The warmth of colorful, naive folk art—the antithesis of sophistication—can humanize the slickest, most upscale contemporary space. Even though these collectibles, at first glance, seem more appropriate for a country interior, they can work equally well, with perhaps even more dramatic impact, in an entirely different, unexpected setting.

Collections can enhance the style and lines of a room, as this collection of art glass heightens the clean, contemporary spareness of this space.

© Eric Roth

Collect with a Consideration to Mood

Collectibles aren't faceless: their presence can change the way a space feels. Collect only those things that enhance the mood you want to create in your home or apartment.

If you want to create a serene atmosphere, the cacophony of primary-colored folk art carvings, with their bold, vibrant paints and often bizarre forms, is diametrically opposed to your goal. A monochromatic collection—perhaps glassware or pottery of a single color and no pattern—that blends with the space instead of clamoring for attention is more appropriate for your needs.

Suppose the mood you want to establish is one of light-hearted gaiety. A collection of pewter may meet your space requirements because of the relatively small scale of its individual pieces, but it does little to evoke a carefree feeling. A collection of small-scale antique toys or whimsical whirligigs, on the other hand, suggests nothing if not fun and childlike escapism.

Opposite page: A collection of quilts stacked at the foot of a bed is both a logical display solution and a dynamic decorative touch. *Above left:* The crystal bottles and elegant figurines atop this table intensify the mood of this room. *Left:* There is nothing formal about a collection of matted and framed art propped against the wall without benefit of hanging, and the collector chose this display technique exactly in order to evoke the casual, contemporary mood of this bedroom.

Collect to Fit Available Space

In addition to collecting the things you love with attention to blending with your home's style and enhancing a desired mood, at least one practical concern must be addressed: space.

If you live in a tiny apartment or cramped loft, a collection of massive antique furniture is not a feasible collectible for you. One of the beauties of collecting, however, is that collectibles that help express your personality come in all sizes and shapes.

For example, a small home featured in one of my magazine articles managed to convey one-of-a-kind character through collections despite its cubicle size. Charming vignettes were created at the home's windowsills using collections of tiny antique inkwells in various shapes, sizes, and materials. Other small collections—old dice, marbles, and other small game materials—graced tabletops. This home smacked of individuality, thanks to these collections, and was every bit as interesting as many larger homes I've written about for publication.

Conversely, if you live in a more spacious home, there really are no size restrictions on your collecting. If circa-1800 painted cupboards are your passion, you can freely indulge, as long as you plan your room designs around your collections.

Above: When the dimensions of a room are given careful consideration beforehand, even a bland bathroom can become an aesthetic delight—here, vintage advertising pieces fill the small bathroom with color and life. *Right:* Collectibles demanding considerable space are limited to a comparably large space. In the right environment, however, these large pieces can provide all the character necessary in a space.

Resolve Size Disputes before Buying

While it's important to be realistic about the general scale of a collection and whether or not there is available space to accommodate it, it is also wise to consider the size of the individual pieces within a collection. One oddball size may pose unforeseen difficulties in displaying your collection.

Suppose you've thought about the limited space in your home for collections, for example, and have decided that a collection of handmade knives would be ideal for you, easily fitting within the available space. Because of knives' relatively small size, you could collect a large number without any danger of encroaching on the living space of your home. But what happens if one knife that is especially appealing, both in appearance and price, is much, much larger than the others you have in mind to collect? Should you buy it?

Ultimately, if you love the knife enough, of course you should. But if you're waffling, think first about how the new piece would look with the rest—and whether it would even physically fit into your display space.

If your knives are displayed, say, on a long console table in your entry hall, the new addition would physically fit and might even provide a visual breath of fresh air, breaking up the stuffiness that can accompany too much homogeneity.

But should your display area be a small, square glass-box store case, the larger knife obviously would not fit. You need to ask yourself, in this case, what would be the point of owning it if you can't display it along with the rest of your collection.

Be honest with yourself. Do you really like the knife enough to have it stand alone, elsewhere in your home? Would it look strangely incongruous? Does it seem to be impossible to integrate the knife anywhere in the home, in which case you would have to resort to storing it away in a drawer, cabinet, or closet?

Discovering that you have invested in a collectible that you can't even keep on view in your home can't help but rankle. Ask any veteran collector. We've all been there. Each time you stumble across your purchase stashed away in a closet is irritating. Most collectors would call the purchase, under these circumstances, a mistake. Anticipating the dilemma before buying the collectible is the only sure way to prevent frustration.

Building More than One Collection

Collecting is akin to a fever. Once the bug is caught, it permeates the system, rising to a plateau before tapering off. Because of the nature of collecting, it is not at all unusual for the collector, on fire with pulling together one collection, to suddenly have the urge to begin new collections in other fields. (The fact is, collecting really does spread like a contagion. I've encountered numerous couples, of whom only one started out as a collector. The other, usually aloof about or even contemptuous of collecting at the outset, became a convert—often pursuing the objects even more zealously than the original collector.)

The question then becomes not how to get started collecting, but how to be sure the next area of collectibles will visually coexist well in the same space as the original collection. What should the next area of collectibles be?

The only rule worth following here is purely intuitive in nature: Build all subsequent collections with the same eye you employed in accumulating the first collection. When the same sensibilities dictate disparate purchases, even the most unrelated objects will blend harmoniously in the home.

As this eclectic mix of pieces shows, multiple collections can be displayed to great effect within a single room, provided that the various collections are somehow related in theme, design, texture, or style.

© Balthazar Korab

Narrowing the Focus

As your sophistication as a collector increases, you may find that your growing discernment doesn't simply mean a narrower range in terms of quality. Certainly you are far less willing to settle for second or third best, but chances are also good that the broad scope your collection initially encompassed may have contracted.

For example, a collector of Staffordshire pottery figurines may initially purchase whatever pieces appeal—Toby jugs, courtship figures, spiel holders of cheerfully colored animals and people. With time, however, that comprehensive range may shrink to include only one of these categories; Toby jugs may now exclusively captivate the collector.

Or it may be that the spectrum of collectibles becomes even more finely focused, with only the pieces of a specific potter—Ralph Waldon, for instance—intriguing the collector.

As the collector matures in this fashion, the market of viable collectibles is dramatically reduced. There are simply fewer pieces available, and those rare pieces that do exist are hard to come by, most being found in the collections of museums or private owners who are not eager to sell.

The irony for the collector is clear: The more he grows in sophistication, the less his collection grows, for his greater knowledge and higher standards have placed him outside the realm of most available collectibles.

Right: An old U.S. mailbox unit holds a mix of small figurines and other collectibles. *Opposite page:* As the collector's taste matures, the field of collecting may narrow—from Christmas decorations in general, for example, to only one form of Christmas ornament, the Nutcracker.

Keep in mind, then, that when you become extremely demanding about what is collectible for you, you may have to sacrifice at least one dimension of collecting: quantity. Most seasoned collectors are happy to jettison numbers for what they gain in the trade: a smaller collection of truly stellar pieces.

When collectors find their interests narrowing from the general to the specific within a given genre of collectibles, the usual solution is to upgrade—sell the pieces in the collection that are no longer of significant interest and use the money to purchase far fewer but more fitting collectibles.

CHAPTER FOUR

DISPLAYING
COLLECTIBLES

As a child born to collecting parents, I might never have rebelled and been inclined to reject collecting had my parents refined their solutions to displaying their beloved objects. Instead, our family home was a jumble with unrelated objects hung, stacked, or strewn seemingly anywhere available space could be found.

Antique leaded crystal from Germany and Italian majolica shared tabletop space with primitive Filipino carvings in my parents' home. English nineteenth-century pen-and-ink lithographs hung next to my father's Western art. A Biedermeier chest was surrounded by various pieces of colonial furniture. The design directive seemed to be overwhelmingly "anything goes."

While such freewheeling eclecticism can produce the liveliest and most interesting of all spaces, even this decorating style must heed certain parameters if chaos is to be avoided. The fact is, no matter how wonderful a collection may be, unless it is properly displayed, it won't have much power to arrest and please viewers.

© Gwendolen Cates

Call to Order

The abiding rule in displaying collections is to create order. Careful planning before arranging collectibles can make the difference in the impact of a space—whether identical displays appear dynamically creative or dreadfully cluttered.

All of a Kind or Kindred Spirits

Order can be attained in two ways: by displaying only like objects—that is, all of a collection displayed together—or by juxtaposing a few pieces of a collection with other objects that share a kindred style, look, or ambience. One of the first decisions that must be made in bringing order, then, is whether it would be more interesting for a collection to be displayed by itself or with other objects related in feel.

If your collection consists of ten earthenware vessels, primitive in style, do you want to display all ten together or break up the collection into two or three individual groupings, to which you add other kinds of primitive objects, such as old wicker baskets or pewter candlesticks? Which approach would command the most attention and be most pleasing to the eye?

If the earthenware pieces vary in size and shape, enough diversity may be present to preclude the need for display with other kinds of accessories. But if the ten items are basically alike in shape and size, with only subtle dissimilarities, it may be advantageous to opt for breaking up the collection into smaller display groups, which include other pieces that can draw the eye with their diversity of scale and height.

Previous page: These ship models are arranged in an effective, one-of-a-kind display that simulates their passage down a long channel. *Left:* A collection of old barbershop tonic bottles and shaving cream mugs. The mugs were personalized with the names and occupations of each customer. The collectors keep this collection, one of the largest of its kind, in an old glass-doored bookcase that keeps dust out and helps prevent breakage caused by casual handling. *Right:* Old typewriters, arranged by size, present a pleasing picture.

Color and Style

If the mix-and-match technique is deemed best, be sure those items chosen for display along with the collectibles are strongly related to the collection in some visual sense. Adding brightly colored, shiny majolica vases to a display group of subtle, matte-textured earthenware because they add a nice touch of height would be a mistake. Though majolica is also pottery and does have a certain peasant quality, it is not as primitive or rustic as the natural-colored earthenware. Other handcrafted wares, in different mediums, can be found that blend more harmoniously with the earthenware. And if crafted pieces such as old wicker baskets or pewter candlesticks aren't appealing, look to nature—to "found" objects, such as speckled cobblestones, sinewy driftwood, or even bird eggs. These natural pieces share the same tonal properties as earthenware, and they are homogeneously organic.

Texture

In addition to sharing compatible color and style, items in a display should relate in texture, too. If the collection's texture is rough, those objects joining it in a display should be rough-textured as well. But beyond this general similarity, pieces will be more interesting if there is some diversity in the specific form taken by the texture.

For example, an ostrich egg with its bumpy surface is rough, but that rough texture is still quite different from the roughness of a piece of bark or rusted barbed wire. Or consider porcelain and glass; both are smooth, but the degree and quality of the smoothness are different. Coupling these kinds of similar, but discrete, textures is more interesting than composing a still life with objects that are identical to the touch.

Sometimes, the most exciting role of texture involves a blend of objects with startlingly different tactile qualities. Trying this marriage of opposites requires some skill, however—a kind of aesthetic sixth sense for knowing when it will work and when it will not. Smooth, nearly slippery chrome Deco cocktail shakers, water pitchers, teapots, and other household collectibles contrast significantly with gritty stoneware from the same era, but the gross difference is no reason to consider combining the two. On the other hand, a smooth contemporary glass bowl is diametrically opposite, in texture (and vintage), from ridged, crumbly seashell fossils— but when the rough, ancient fossils are encased in the slick modern bowl, somehow, the union works. Trial and error is the only way to develop an astute intuition for when it is appropriate to join disparate textures.

Opposite page: Beaded bags look stunning laid flat on their backs on a display surface that is simple and noncompetitive. ***Left:*** The curved shapes and varying heights of the dinosaurs create a sense of movement in this arrangement.

Limit Mixed Groups

When augmenting a collection with additional kinds of objects to heighten interest in the arrangement, be careful to limit the number of pieces in any still life you create. Include enough of the collectible items in any one grouping to convey the idea that this is a collection, but don't go overboard. Choose wisely and limit the number of pieces to be displayed.

Likewise, the additional objects to be displayed with the collection will inject interest only when used judiciously, in moderation. When juxtaposing collectibles with other accessories, too many collectibles or too many additional objects will sabotage all efforts at creating order. Therefore, the best advice when displaying a mixed group of kindred spirits is to divide the collection into discrete display groups, to minimize confusion.

Heighten Small Collections

If a collection consists of extremely small pieces, you may want to mix some other, taller objects with it. Small objects on a tabletop tend to get lost visually, while other areas of the room in which there are taller objects become the focal points instead. Certainly this is true if the collection is not only small in size but also in number.

To give a collection of small objects the attention it deserves, experiment with different kinds of groupings. Try clustering the diminutive collectibles on a small table with an appropriate lamp. (Lighting, to be discussed in greater detail later, is an important decorating tool that can determine whether a collection gets full attention.) Or try adding several other objects of varying heights and shapes to serve as visual steps, making the leap of eye to the small collectibles gradual, natural, and hardly discernible.

Right: Small collectibles get lost when mixed with larger pieces. To give diminutive objects maximum attention, mass them together; there is power in numbers.

Opposite page: The most exciting displays are those that are most unusual. Try mirroring the shape of the display surface in the design of the collection, as the arrangement of these car models are patterned after the circular shape of the table.

Power in Numbers

Sometimes, especially with collections that have grown extremely large, the most impact will be achieved through a display that capitalizes on sheer volume—arranging the collectibles, one after the other, on and on, in a single space. In this situation, no additional accessories or objets d'art are necessary. The monotony of the pieces ironically becomes a riveting attraction in itself, the magnetic draw being repetition.

Balance

One of the problems many homeowners have shared with me in my capacity as a design writer is their frustration in attempting to create interesting arrangements of accessories. From what I've been able to ascertain, the problem boils down to balance. People are displeased with their efforts at making beautiful still lifes, feeling that something is "just not right" because the final effort is somehow not balanced.

Collections may be art or objets d'art, but no matter how fine, they are still accessories and are still susceptible to the same kind of mistakes in arranging. Displays of collectibles must be balanced if the overall look is to be charming and orderly.

Balance can be achieved in two ways: symmetrically or asymmetrically. For the aficionado of order, a symmetrical arrangement may be more pleasing. This is the kind of balance in which, were a plumb line to be dropped down the center of a display, the two halves would be mirror images of one another.

A more spontaneous look is possible with asymmetrical arrangements of collectibles—two tall pieces, perhaps, at the right end of a display surface, balanced by a mass of shorter but more numerous objects to the left.

When arrangements are neither symmetrical nor asymmetrical but merely random placements of objects with no attention to height or weight (the visual bulk of an object or several closely grouped objects), the absence of balance prohibits a sense of cohesion. Confusion is substituted for order.

Opposite page and left: This collection of snow domes from around the world attracts attention through the power of its numbers. Smaller collectibles that might be overpowered when displayed atop a table among larger pieces become more of a focal point when they fill the inside of a glass-front cabinet, with nothing to distract.

Front and Center vs. Silhouette

Different objects require a different presentation based on their inherent qualities. Some sculptural pieces are shown to their best advantage in silhouette, while other objects command fullest attention when viewed head on.

A collection of slat-back Shaker chairs can be hung upside down on pegboard (in the authentic manner of the original Shaker communities) and be stunningly visual. The simplicity of the chairs' straight, clean lines enables this kind of presentation.

But for a collection of early children's chairs with bent, undulating backs, this kind of head-on, upside-down display would be devastating to the chairs' integrity. For this collection, the profile is the point of pride. The chairs would be better displayed on special shelving with enough width to accommodate the chairs turned sideways, to draw the eye immediately to their sculptural silhouettes.

Common sense dictates that the best display is the one in which the individual items are all clearly visible from their most important vantage point. In a collection of antique toys that encompasses a wide range of designs and forms, each piece should not necessarily be displayed in the same way. A whirligig or perhaps a toy train or stagecoach may look best from the side view, which captures its elongated shape. A Steiff teddy bear, by contrast, requires a frontal presentation if all of its features are to be seen. Some large antique children's books can be laid flat, while a book with one contiguous page that unfolds, accordion style, must be displayed upright and open. Whatever the collection, allow the inherent design of the individual pieces to influence their display.

Above: Old machinist's surface gauges rest, appropriately, atop a machinists' tool chest with drawers ajar to reveal other tools in the collection. *Right:* By cleverly arranging these machinists' leveling jacks on a chessboard, the collector has highlighted their resemblance to chess pieces, making for a surprising and appealing display.

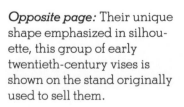

Opposite page: Their unique shape emphasized in silhouette, this group of early twentieth-century vises is shown on the stand originally used to sell them.

Ups and Downs

Like the regular children's book and the folding one, different collectibles appear to their best advantage either standing upright or lying down. Quilts obviously take on a totally different appearance when opened up and hung on the wall, instead of being folded and stacked flat. The entirety of the design, intricacy of the pattern, and quality of the workmanship become clearly visible. But unless your desire is to have an entire room or space pivot on the wall-displayed quilt (or quilts), this much impact is undesirable. (Wall space, too, becomes a real concern when the quilt collection is large.) The desired effect must determine the choice of display.

A collection of women's high-heeled shoes, based on their design, could easily be hung by the heels in a display. But what would the viewer actually see? A gaping hole that is the hollow interior of the shoe. In this instance, a better solution would be one that presents the shoes either in silhouette (if space permits) or from the front.

Untouchables

With some collectibles, a decision needs to be made as to whether the collection is for open display or whether, on account of its frailty or the likelihood of its getting damaged, it should be contained under glass.

This decision is especially important when the collection is ephemeral, that is, of materials that do not intrinsically have longevity (paper or textile collectibles, such as the highly collectible, colorful cigar-box illustrations, for example). Do you want to risk ripping, creasing, or otherwise damaging the ephemeral collection, or even having it crumble from simple exposure? To protect your paper or small, fragile textiles (family needlework, lace, and the like) consider either a wall or shelf display that covers the pieces with a sheer layer of non-glare glass.

Opposite page and left: Balance must be considered in any room display incorporating collectibles. Here, the visual weight of the painting is balanced by the strong vertical line of the lamp, providing a frame for the glass-encased collections. Viewed from up close, this still-life arrangement is seen to include hatpins, antique dolls, pocket knives, watch faces, a dish with a photo, and a jade cup. These delicate collectibles are kept safe from handling in an old candy store display case with a mirrored back, circa 1910.

A Room with a View

One of the concerns that worries many new collectors is selecting the best room for displaying the pieces. Should collections, which represent a considerable investment of time, money, and self-expression, be displayed only in the most public spaces of the home? Is it appropriate to present soft collectibles in hard spaces? Are certain rooms off limits as showcases for collections? The following recommendations are intended as starting points—foolproof solutions. Do not stop with them, however. Read on to chapter 6 for more unusual—and fun—approaches.

The issue of public versus private spaces can be handily dismissed. Important collections that are a clear articulation of the collector's interests and personality obviously mean the most when displayed in a setting in which they have the greatest visibility and exposure. Only a privacy fanatic would consider banishing a collection of rare pre-Columbian sculpture to the bedroom if no other collections exist for more public areas.

A central location in the home or apartment is justified for such an important collection. But this does not necessarily mean the living room. The tone of a home is established immediately upon entry. Look to a foyer or formal entry hallway as a possible location for boldly displaying these prime collections.

Another guideline to keep in mind in selecting the right room for a collection is to marry content with context. A collection of spice tins may reflect years of poring over offerings at flea markets and estate sales, but the collection would be sorely out of place in a traditional eighteenth-century living room. The obvious setting for the collection is the kitchen, where it could rest harmoniously on a baker's rack, in an antique cupboard, or atop custom shelving.

Some collections are more personal by nature, lending themselves to the softer, more personal quarters of the home. A textiles collection of old family christening gowns, for instance, with its soft, white fabrics and lace, would blend beautifully in a master bedroom suite with a compatibly subtle, romantic feel. The intimacy of the collection, on the other hand, might be jarringly disturbing in a family room decorated with bold colors and textures and home to loud electronics and a string of visitors.

The decision of where to house a collection often pivots on the extent of the collection. I recall visiting the home of Beverly Fields, a designer who was a compulsive collector of contemporary art. The fact that her son was an artist meant the house possessed an overflowing supply of artwork. Every room of the home, not just the central living space, was filled with dramatic presentations of art. Even the bathroom was a gallery—and a real, unexpected treat for guests.

No room in the home, then, is inappropriate or taboo for displaying a collection. Some of the most unlikely spaces can bring the greatest delight. But for the moderate-sized collection, it is usually best to play it safe, showcasing the most important collections in the most heavily trafficked spaces, and tailor-fitting the choice of display spaces to the objects that are to be displayed.

In this contemporary library, a collection of globes blends harmoniously with the booklined cases.

CHAPTER FIVE

CONTAINMENT

Having determined the room or rooms most suitable for displaying a collection, and having ascertained the most appropriate manner of display, the question becomes more specific: On which particular surface should the collection be presented? As a starting point, a consideration of design styles can identify a few options.

Bear in mind that the options suggested for one design style aren't necessarily exclusive to that style, however. A console table, for example, though suggested as a display area for contemporary collectibles, could also be an excellent receptacle for vintage traditional or country collections, if the design and materials of the console are in some way akin to one of those styles.

Keep in mind, also, that the suggestions offered in this chapter are the most proven, reliable ones. When a professional designer is not being used, it's often comforting to start safe and slowly grow more adventurous. The recommendations given here can allow practitioners to maintain peace of mind, knowing they have committed no major design faux pas; the way in which they have displayed their collections is perfectly acceptable and appropriate. But don't stop with this chapter of conventional approaches to designing with collectibles. The fun of design lies in the unexpected. After wresting some security about your decorating options from this material, turn to chapter 6 to shake things up a bit—for when the pieces resettle, the end result is sure to have more singular verve and snap.

Previous page: Fine collections don't necessarily have to be confined to the living or dining rooms. The hallway may be an excellent location to show a collection, especially, as here, when designed with custom cases or shelving.

Right: Entertainment centers allow ample display space for collections like these "carnival art" chalk figures from the 1930s and '40s, which at one time were commonly given away at county fairs and carnivals.

© Ed Wolff

Contemporary

Contemporary collectibles, such as vibrantly colored pottery by today's talented clay artists, or even collectibles as understated and elegantly simple as pale Chinese celadon, demand a suitably subtle, monochromatic background as a foil for showing off the collection to the greatest advantage. The best possibilities include contemporary case goods, consoles, custom shelving, and niches—architectural solutions that preserve the clean lines of the room, underscoring the importance of good bones as the key element of the overall design.

Case Goods

If the room is rectilinear with ample wall space and if there is a desire to avoid the major changes of new construction that custom shelving or niches would entail, case goods are the option that first come to mind for holding a contemporary collection. These pieces, because of their scale and placement across a wall, are more architectural than other types of freestanding furnishings. They permit plenty of air in the center of the room, which is vital to contemporary design's requirement of openness, spareness, and absence of clutter.

Entertainment centers—wall case goods with a combination of open and closed (cabinet) shelving, that can be stacked side by side—are readily available from nearly every manufacturer of contemporary furniture. These can be ideal for displaying a collection because the collector can purchase as many or as few individual units as necessary, but the shelving itself is generally flexible, open to whatever arrangement according to number and height of shelves the buyer desires.

A collection can occupy each shelf of the unit or can be strategically placed on alternating shelves, with another type of collection or other compatible objets d'art filling the other spaces. Books work especially well coexisting on entertainment centers with a collection. And it stands to reason that the primary function of the unit—housing home electronics such as TV, VCR, and sound system—can also be fulfilled, while using the remaining shelves for a collection.

If you elect to have the lower shelves closed behind cabinet doors, this area serves as an out-of-sight cache for anything from magazines to CDs—efficient storage space that permits a clean, uncluttered look for the overall room.

The cabineted areas can also house finely orchestrated displays or collectibles. Not every possession has to be on exhibit 100 percent of the time. Collections not in use on the upper shelves still can be arranged in an aesthetically pleasing fashion behind doors. You may wish to alternate the collections, putting away displayed items and bringing out the stored pieces, to give a dramatic new look to the room.

Contemporary wall case goods such as entertainment centers are compatible with contemporary collections because the furniture is streamlined, with no gratuitous decorative furbelows—no carvings, turnings, or finials—that would detract from the simple but bold design of the collection. The collection itself, without competition, can stand as the pièce de résistance of the space.

Another advantage of case goods is that they are available in a variety of finishes. Natural wood finishes might be desirable for a collection such as new birch baskets or American Indian kachinas, which have an earthier, more rustic feeling. Black lacquer is a dramatic background for a collection of contemporary art glass—especially when proper attention is paid to lighting. White lacquer, similarly, shows off darker collectibles to their best advantage. For a more colorful presentation, finishes can be selected from many other colors.

Consoles

Consoles are a highly flexible solution for the display of contemporary collections. Like case goods, console tables can be purchased directly off the showroom floor. Unlike large, tall entertainment centers or shelving, however, consoles can fit into almost any existing space—in an entry hall, against a dining room wall, or even behind a sofa in the living room.

Consoles are available in more unusual and interesting designs than can be found in entertainment centers. A variety of textures and finishes are offered, from smooth glass, slick lacquer, and different types of marble to rougher woods, faux finishes over wood, grainy stone, or even hard iron, aluminum, brass, chrome, or nickel. Each of these is suitable for some kind of contemporary collection, and the diversity of offerings means that a collection and the console that contains it can be closely related in style and texture.

One possible disadvantage of consoles should be acknowledged: limited display area. If a collection is extremely large, the console table probably will not be able to accommodate the entire collection all at once. In this case, pieces can be alternated, which keeps the display fresh and interesting. But if for some reason that's unacceptable, another solution should be considered.

Opposite page: Victorian jewelry is on display but safe from handling in this console table.

Custom Shelving

Building shelving to house a collection obviously requires more effort than purchasing ready-made shelving off the showroom floor and, for that reason, is not an option for those wishing to avoid the additional time and trouble. For collectors who do not own their own homes, custom shelving also is not advised, as the investment has a limited life span, remaining with the residence as a permanent part of the architecture when the collector moves on.

But if the conditions are right for building shelving, this display solution is often best, because shelves can be built to precise specifications to accommodate the individual pieces of the collection. Smaller collectibles, or those that are generally uniform in size, can be housed on shelves of one height. For a larger piece or pieces, a niche can be built in the shelves. These niches should be planned carefully to ensure balance. A niche on the left side, for example, needs to be balanced by a niche on the right, although the location doesn't have to be exactly symmetrical. Balance can be achieved by locating one niche high and another low. Look carefully at drawings before proceeding with construction.

Besides allowing a tailored fit to the specific pieces in a collection, custom shelving offers some other advantages. It creates architecture in a room where there may be none. Also, because the shelving is a fixed, integral part of the room, not freestanding, it is more versatile for furniture placement: chairs or sofas can be pulled up close to the shelving to create a conversation area without the crowded or seemingly awkward sense such an arrangement could have if attempted with a freestanding furniture wall unit.

One more benefit of custom shelving is that it can span the full width and height of the wall, creating a seamless look in the interior design.

Finally, the special shelves designed to accommodate a collection can be blended exactly in coloration to the remainder of the room's palette, if that is desired, for an easy-on-the-eye uniformity in decor. This is not the only color solution possible, however.

Above: Custom shelving is the perfect solution for this mix of colorful collectibles and books. *Opposite page:* A collection of pots has riveting impact when each one is displayed in an individual custom niche, with backlighting. The niche wall becomes almost a piece of sculpture in its own right.

The back of the shelves may be painted the same color as the rest of the room, while the shelves themselves can be done in another hue extracted from the room's color scheme. For a collection of black-and-white pottery, for example, the custom shelves may be designed to repeat both colors. Caution should be exercised with color, however. Too much injudicious daring can be self-defeating, creating a clamor that dilutes the impact of the collection.

Best of Both Worlds

If custom shelving is dismissed as a possibility but the architectural look of built-ins is desired, there is a compromise. Place freestanding entertainment components across the wall in the arrangement you want, then connect them to the ceiling with molding that matches that in the remainder of the room. Adhere matching molding across the bottom of the case goods, making them seamless with the floor. (The molding you use for this wall treatment may be the only such detail in the room. As such, it's your opportunity to show a little architectural flair.)

To create even more of a built-in look, leave some space between the cabinets, then connect the individual units with the same molding you used for the top of the furnishings. (This molding could even be plain laminant board, to maintain the sparse look of the contemporary design.) This compromise allows the look of built-ins with only a fraction of the work. The down side, of course, is that the "wall" must be disassembled whenever you want the cabinets moved—with whatever damage to the case goods that might entail.

Niches

One of the most beautiful and sophisticated display surfaces for contemporary (and other) collections is niches. Small, interior grottos of sorts, these spaces differ from custom shelving in that they are recessed into the wall, rather than projected out from it. Niches are concave; shelving is convex.

Niches provide a dramatic treatment for a collection that numbers only a few pieces, or for the highlights of a larger collection. They are especially good for displaying sculpture. Whatever the collectible, though, the effect is greatest when the niches are used sparingly in a space. Too many, and the look will not be dynamic and arresting but cluttered and confusing. Niches, then, clearly are not intended as warehouses for a large collection in its entirety.

Of all the options for contemporary displays, niches are the most complex to implement. Existing walls must be extended with studs and drywall to create room for the recesses, which will have the original wall as their backs. This means totally reshaping the bones of a room or at least one of its walls. Therefore, unless the collector is committed to undertaking such a major overhaul, at peace with the time and expense as well as with the reduced usable square footage for the room that it entails, niches would better remain outside the realm of real possibilities.

Should the investment of effort be deemed viable, however, niches can bring much pleasure, not only as unusual receptacles for collectibles, but as architectural additions of major significance. Although custom shelving heightens the architectural interest of a room, carefully situated niches go even further, evoking stunning effects. When properly lit, the niche is without peer as a presentation area.

Country

The country design style, with its amazing eclecticism and mix of old and new elements, affords one of the most open-ended—and creative—solutions for the display of collections. Naive, early rural furnishings with their imperfections, free-form and exuberant style, and, often, original chipped paint in old colors such as oxblood, mustard, or buttermilk blue, present an excellent opportunity for showcasing a country collection of similar style and period.

A cheerfully mixed display of country collectibles.

Should the desired antiques be hard to find or prohibitively expensive, however, the good news in this design style is that there is a plethora of well-made reproductions on the market at more affordable prices. Each year, major furnishing manufacturers are increasing their country offerings either with reproductions and/or adaptations of early pieces, or with whimsical country designs that aren't intended to look old but stand firmly on their own merits as contemporary country folk art. Often, these latter pieces incorporate rustic materials or special decorative-paint finishes such as trompe l'oeil, stenciling, sponging, stippling, or any number of attractive faux finishes.

Whereas contemporary collectibles are fairly limited in the types of areas on which they may be displayed, country collections are not. The quirky, folksy nature of country design means that an unlimited number of odd, offbeat furnishings can be employed to display collections. Use your imagination. Some suggestions for unusual country displays will be provided in chapter 6. For mainstream displaying, consider the following country staples.

Cupboards, Corner Cabinets, Pie Safes

Tall, wooden storage furnishings are a mainstay of country design. In early homes, cupboards were located in the kitchen, dining room, or keeping room (and many of the homes had only one of these spaces, not all three) as storehouses for the family's china, stoneware, pewter, and other household utensils. The reason was simple: early kitchens did not have the luxury of wall-to-wall, built-in cabinetry. In addition to a closeted area usually located in the lower half, these cupboards often had an open display section at the top, which is where most of today's collectors concentrate their pieces.

Most of these antique American country cupboards are circa nineteenth century, though some still can be found from the late eighteenth century. Antique primitive cupboards from England and Ireland or Europe, especially Scandinavia, also work beautifully in country spaces. The cabinets typically are executed in a plain wood such as pine.

Opposite page, above: Old metal advertising pieces are among the most popular country collectibles. *Left:* On the left edge of this photograph can be seen a corner cupboard holding a china collection; on the right, the visual play of miniature chests aligned on the stairway makes a trip up the stairs more exciting.

Left: Country collectibles have a special charm that is enhanced when the collection is displayed in a country cupboard that may itself be collectible. *Right:* Old spice tins make for colorful, whimsical collectibles that add warmth to any style of decor.

CONTAINMENT

79

Especially prized among country antiques aficionados are those cupboards still wearing their original coat of paint. With these, perfection is not the issue: the greater the chipping and visible wear and tear, the more charming the piece.

Country collectors prize cupboards as prime display areas for their collections. Although such furnishings were originally intended to hold everyday dinnerware or finer china and crystal to be used on special occasions, today these pieces are seldom kept in the cupboards. Instead, they hold those special collections that demand attention—early salt glaze, Bennington or Pfaltzgraff pottery, spongeware, splatterware, or any other of a multitude of collecting choices not intended for actual use.

In most of today's well-designed country homes, at least one cupboard can be found in every kitchen, dining room, and living room. These tall furnishings add needed height to the rooms, and are thus important design elements in themselves. Their inclusion in different rooms permits the display of different types of collectibles, the most formal typically going in the living or dining room cupboards and the least formal in the cabinet in the kitchen. (But this logical placement of formal with formal, casual with casual, is not the only, or even necessarily the best, solution. A collection of redware plates can look great in the living room, as well as [more traditionally] in the dining room or kitchen. Flow pottery can work in a family room. To prove the point, just consider birdhouses—pieces originally intended for outdoors that are now among the hottest indoor collectibles.)

Corner cabinets, those constructed at a ninety-degree angle to turn the corner at an end of a room, are a variation of the country cupboard. The display area is usually somewhat more limited in these pieces (like cupboards, the top portion of the cabinet is generally open shelving and the lower is closed behind a door), but they can be excellent containers for a small group of collectibles such as candlesticks or perhaps a few cups and saucers. A matched set of corner cabinets placed at either corner of one end of a room creates

balance and a nicely finished effect. These pieces can also be the answer when corners would otherwise be dead spaces, inadequate for the placement of a standard cupboard or other type of furnishing. Corner cabinets—more elegant display spaces than regular cupboards—are generally placed in a more formal space such as the dining room.

Pie safes, the most casual country cabinets, are traditionally considered more appropriate as an element of interest in the kitchen. The top of the pie safe serves as one display space for a relatively small collection or vignette of collectibles, while inside affords storage space for a larger collection. Even though the top half of the pie safe is usually closed behind a decoratively pierced tin door, it makes a charming display when one of the doors is propped open.

Chimney Cupboards

One type of country cabinet, the chimney cupboard, merits separate mention. This tall, slender cupboard, usually crafted from beadboard, is not a stellar piece of furniture as much as an ideal solution to a tight squeeze—a space too small for nearly any other type of furniture. Small collectibles such as miniature wood houses find ample breathing room upon this cottage-size cupboard.

Behind Closed Doors

A final point—one that should be underlined and starred—needs to be made on country cabinets as a whole, as caches for collectibles: As much as it may sound like heresy, especially to the neophyte collector, there is no etched-in-stone design rule that says that cabinets necessarily must be open to contain interesting displays.

Ceramic dishes shaped like fruits and vegetables are popular among collectors. Displayed in a kitchen or dining room cupboard, they lend a colorful charm to the decor.

© Eric Roth

The excitement of interior design lies in the unexpected, in whatever surprises—such as a collection within a closed cabinet—a home can offer. This approach keeps the home interesting not only for guests, who are treated to surprises, but for the homeowners themselves.

When every collectible is presented in full view all the time, the home becomes predictable; soon it feels stale and the owner wants a change, which usually means some degree of redecorating.

The beauty of designing a home with collections is that change can be executed, and a feeling of freshness and vitality maintained, simply through good stewardship of the collectibles and their display treatments. What could be more fun than passing by a country cabinet in the dining room that's been closed for a couple of weeks, opening the door, and discovering a beautiful still life of folk-art log cabins? Left open, it might prove too much rusticity to deal with, day in and day out, but could be a great visual treat occasionally. Or peeking in the cupboard to find a well-organized presentation of heirloom lace and linens that are best protected from dust and sunlight, but still a source of delight that deserves good design, not mere warehousing?

Not only does displaying collectibles behind closed doors serve as a practical solution to many collections that, for some reason, don't lend themselves to permanent, open exhibition, it is also a design treatment that brings greater depth and completion to the home.

Traditional

More than any other design, traditional style relies on furnishings to communicate its message. An eighteenth-century Philadelphia highboy, with its fine veneer, elegant finials and pediment, and scallop shell carving on the apron,

Right: China need not always be displayed in the dining room— it can add interest to other rooms, as well, as in this traditional living room.

creates its own architectural statement in a room, especially considering the piece's height. In the best traditional rooms, the furniture itself is the most significant collection.

This differs from contemporary design, in which furnishings often are minimal in size and style; architecture, more than furniture, is the canvas on which the contemporary portrait is painted. Traditional design's emphasis on furnishings differs from the country design genre, too, which draws its character most heavily from a freestyle use of accessories—collections, folk art, an offbeat item such as an old sarsaparilla box or a piece of vintage leather luggage.

With traditional design, then, unlike the other two decorating styles, collectibles must be carefully integrated into a room with consideration, first, to furniture. Never

Below: Antique tools positioned on this paneled wall behind a dry sink are as intriguing as any framed piece of art.

should the collections detract from the furnishings. They must be chosen and displayed to complement and underscore the larger pieces. The option of creating architectural display areas for collections through manufactured or custom wall units, as with contemporary design, is less important in traditional spaces. The flexibility of country's approach to collectibles is substituted in traditional design with a more studied formality.

Tabletops

The starting point for designing with collectibles in a traditional room is the existing furnishings, with the assumption that these pieces have merit and that new additions for the sole purpose of housing collectibles are not necessarily desirable. A staple furnishing in the traditional room is the table, which knows endless variety, from the small tea table to the larger game table, on to the more desklike library table, the writing table, the pier table, and the sideboard. Traditional tables can be highly specialized, too, as attested by the flap-top harlequin table, shaving table, and wine table. Each of these table surfaces provides an important resolution to the problem of where to show collectibles in a traditional room.

Collectibles displayed atop tables must be of a scale proportionate to that of the furniture. Avoid placing very large objects, even if only a few of them, on small tables. The scale of the collection will overpower the furnishing, and the mass of the collectibles is likely to obscure the table's polished finish or its marble veins. Allow the table to be dominant, like a tree, with the collectibles as branches and leaves.

Most tables in traditional rooms are intended to serve some function, usually as handy places to stash a glass or cup, or as a source of reading or room light. Allow some space on the table for the primary functions to be fulfilled. When a lamp is needed on the table, be sure it is compatible with the collection—or that the collection is compatible with it.

Above: You don't have to execute major architectural changes to a room or purchase special pieces to prominently display a collection. Tabletops are enhanced by small collections while still functioning as light sources or surfaces for a book or cup of tea.
Opposite page: Any home with a fireplace mantel has natural display space. This collection of candlesticks banked on a mantel lend the room luminous charm.

Secretaries and Cabinets

Without a doubt, the most magnificent pieces in traditional rooms are the tall case goods. While the king of these furnishings, the highboy, does not contain open display space for collections, most other pieces do: a pedimented combination bureau-bookcase, secretary, or more slender ladies' desk, drawing-room cabinet, china cabinet, or bookcase. As with traditional tables, care must be taken to select and arrange collections on these case goods in a way complementary to, not competitive with, the furnishing itself.

Mantels

Although furniture is the single most important element in a traditional room and therefore the best place to start when considering where to show collectibles, the mantel is another extremely important space for this function. Mantels in traditional homes are beautiful architectural features, often with neoclassical entablatures or other examples of rich molding. The mantel shelf, guaranteed to draw attention on its own merits, understandably becomes a favorite place for presenting a collection that bears showing off.

A collection of period silver candlesticks easily fits the narrow depth of the mantel, as do small leather-bound books, vases, and framed photographs. The possibilities of collectibles that can be pleasingly displayed on the mantel are limitless. Take care to limit the number of items included, however. Use only enough to convey the idea of a collection. Otherwise, the space will become cluttered and detract not only from the collection but from the rest of the room as well.

A Classic Pitfall

Collections in traditional homes often reflect the extensive travels of the owners, rather than hours of browsing in nearby flea markets (as with country collectibles) or following the works of certain artisans and artists (as with contemporary collections). Ironically, the potential for chaos in homes designed with collections thus becomes greater in traditional homes—which should be paragons of order—than in either of the other decorating fields.

From a trip to the East, the traditional collector may return home laden with a trunk filled with cloisonné, cinnabar, celadon, and jade, with larger chinoiserie furnishings to be shipped home. A visit to Portugal may mean additions of peasant-style water jugs and decorative glassware bearing that country's traditional folk-art motif of the rooster—all somehow to be worked into rooms containing the collections from the Orient. A stop in Ireland can produce enough Waterford crystal to form its own iceberg; England for silver; India for bronzes and brass.

It's not hard to see how bringing order to such a menagerie of objects could be a forbidding challenge, especially when the decorating style is one in which order is imperative and the integrity of the major furnishings under no circumstances can be compromised. It was precisely this travelers' pitfall that left my parents' home in a state of disarray. Never can they travel without returning with entirely new collections or additions to existing ones—and they spend a majority of their time traveling. Unless restraint and order are imposed in such homes, the results are enough to make onlookers sour toward collections in general.

All of a Kind

To avoid confusion in a traditional decor, with a mishmash of fine but unrelated collectibles from all parts of the earth scattered everywhere so that no individual collection musters the attention it deserves, collections must be organized and displayed according to type. Instead of filling the shelves of a secretary with ornate baroque silver, Murano blown glass, German leaded crystal, and South Pacific folk carvings, divide and conquer. Segregate like collections into discrete groups of their own. Limit the display in the secretary to leaded crystal and baroque silver, which share a similar style and have subtle colors and distinct textures that complement one another. Confine a collection as busy as folk carvings, with their multifarious colors and forms, to a display entirely its own, in a portion of a room in which there is little pattern or color or other objects to compete with the collection.

Plan B

When collecting becomes compulsive, with many different individual collections of varying styles all competing for shelf or table space in the traditional room, it's time to implement a different plan: Display only a few collections at a time and store the rest.

Especially with important collections, this is the only way to show them at their best—to ensure that they are even seen at all. If the urge to admire a collection not currently on display should arise, it's simple enough either to get a quick fix by looking at it in its storage area or to savor a more lasting pleasure by retrieving it and returning to storage a collection that has already had its time on view.

Whenever an individual collection grows plentiful or a few collections expand into several, it's a good idea to try Plan B. No one can be expected to respond favorably to possessions when so many are out at one time that the eye can't comfortably study anything or find rest anywhere. By alternating collections, the pieces can be noticed—and the decor of the rooms themselves will continually look fresh and exciting. Collections are the jewels of the traditional home. Imagine the disturbing, diminishing impact of wearing huge diamonds, emeralds, and rubies on each finger of both hands at once. Not only would the display be garish, it would be impossible to fully appreciate any one of the stones, no matter how beautiful, rare, or valuable.

Bulletin boards can show collectibles in a sophisticated adult room.

CHAPTER SIX

EXPLORE THE UNEXPECTED

As much as common sense informs interior design, it is only a partial explanation for a successfully designed space. Good judgment in selecting and mixing color, pattern, texture, scale, and style ensures a room that is pleasing to the eye and in no way offensive; it does not ensure a room that pulsates with creativity and visual excitement. To achieve designs that are not only good but dynamic, more is required: an eye for the unexpected. This design principle holds true for decorating as a whole, and it also applies to designing with collections specifically.

Just as a room with a sofa pulled out from the wall onto the diagonal is more interesting than one in which the sofa rests predictably flush with the wall, a room designed with collections has more spark when the collectibles are unusual and their arrangement and display are innovative.

Sometimes, people designing their own homes or apartments without the aid of a professional feel more comfortable taking the safe, sure route. There's nothing wrong with this approach. But after collections have been mentally, if not physically, integrated into a room's design in a secure but predictable manner, why not pause and rethink the space? Perhaps a portion of one collection can be relocated into an entirely different, less obvious room. Maybe a furnishing you never even considered as housing a collection can be enlisted. It's even possible that, as you assess your possessions, you may find already existing collections you never realized you had among such things as cast-off sporting goods or children's discarded toys. When pulled together in the right display, these can invigorate a bland space that perhaps wasn't even among your original decorating priorities.

Previous page: This metal star collection adds flair to a traditional room. *Right:* A kitchen cabinet for everyday dishes can do double duty housing colorful and eclectic collectibles, including vintage Fiesta and Harlequin dishware, a Czechoslovakian deco vase, Japanese vases, and water pitchers. *Opposite page:* This still life of Teddy Bears shows how a little creativity can transform ordinary objects into an unexpected and delightful collection that lends new life to any room.

© Jennifer Lévy

Forgotten Places

To create zing in your home via designing with collectibles, look to the least likely rooms, nooks, and crannies of the home. Spaces such as the laundry room, garage, hallway, or lackluster guest room all have the potential for making drop-dead design statements.

Experiment at role playing. Imagine yourself as an interior designer you have just contacted to discuss the decorating needs of your home. Walk through your house as though for the first time, seeing it through fresh eyes—the hypothetical eyes of your new designer. Go through each room, even those practically sealed off from the rest of the world. Take mental note of what's in each space and what could be done with it. Try to empty yourself of any preconceptions and hasty conclusions. Evaluate the spaces as they truly are, not as you've grown to typecast them over the years. Does any room stand out as having unmet potential? Do any ideas come to mind for change? The following inventory of overlooked places may help you identify a few of your own.

© Tim Lee

Laundry Rooms

Depending on the part of the country in which you live, the laundry room will look different. In Texas, where temperatures are mild and basements therefore almost nonexistent, laundry or utility rooms are usually located on the main floor of the home. Consequently, these spaces are finished construction, with flooring and drywall or plaster. Beyond this, however, they are seldom given a thought as spaces in need of decorating. Too bad, considering how much time is spent here meeting the laundry needs of an average-size household.

In colder climates, where laundry rooms are usually located in the basement, even less thought is given to these spaces. The rooms frequently retain concrete flooring while walls are unfinished and ceilings expose pipes and wires. Dreary environments, at best, in which to perform a household chore not too popular to begin with.

To bring life to the laundry room, explore the contents of boxes in the attic. Three or four old wood-and-metal scrub boards passed down from your grandmother may turn up among a potpourri of stored items. Take these to the laundry room and mount them on the wall or prop them against an old wooden work bench. The washboards might not be collectibles to which you would want to devote prime living room space, but they can go a long way in transforming the dull laundry room into an area that has at least a glimmer of character.

The more deadly dull the room, the greater the need for an infusion of life. Humor is often the best antidote. Instead of throwing away broken irons, traditional symbols of female labor, try arranging a group of them in the laundry room on a cast-off ironing board. The antique, non-electric irons known as sad irons because of their heavy weight have long been considered collectibles. The newer, electric irons are less likely to be collected and, in my opinion, therefore a bit more interesting.

Mudrooms

On the East Coast, the mudroom (a small room where outdoor gear—coats, boots, sporting equipment—is kept) is a fixture in most homes. Sometimes it is treated as a catchall, with far more than mud spilling into it. In other homes, it's simply neglected space—used, to be sure, but given its rugged, utilitarian performance, not treated with much seriousness as a contender for a single decorating thought. Yet in those homes in which the mudroom is given a fighting chance as a designed space, replete with collections, the results can make it one of the best rooms in the house.

Furniture is not necessary to turn the mudroom into a space with a personality reflective of the rest of the home. Collections can execute the design entirely on their own.

The mudroom's walls can be a repository for old commercial signage—a collection of early, metal soft-drink advertisement signs, wooden store logos, or old-fashioned pharmaceutical ads. Along similar lines, a collection of old metal thermometers displaying brightly painted names of businesses and products works well in the mudroom (a space where the temperature is a point of interest, as it's usually cooler or warmer than in the rest of the home). For another appropriate collecting statement, stack old wooden egg crates or other primitive boxes.

A very simple way to give style to the mudroom is by turning those items naturally located there—shoes, coats, and hats—into collections on display. Hang hats and coats across a wall on pegboard, with attention to color and shape. Create a display of canvas high-top sneakers along the wall.

The mudroom's collections can be seasonally alternated. Arrange sports gear like tennis racquets and fishing nets in displays for the summer, and change the look entirely, come winter, with a display of snowshoes, skis, and sleds.

Why make the laundry room strictly utilitarian? With a few related collectibles such as old-fashioned scrub boards and old boxes of detergent, even this often-ignored space can look lively.

Hallways

The vacant wall space along a long hallway affords a wonderful but usually overlooked opportunity for a gallery-like presentation of collectibles. This space becomes especially important in a tract house, which may lack architectural embellishments of molding, wainscoting, and other trim work that imbue a home with visual interest.

Favorite old black-and-white family photographs that have been hidden away in photo albums or boxes and stashed in the closet can finally receive the space they need, and can be hung en masse in glass-covered frames for a dramatic presentation.

Heirloom quilts for which there is inadequate space elsewhere in the home find plenty of elbowroom in the hall. They add rich color and bold geometric or pictorial design to the hall's otherwise antiseptic walls.

For the serious art collector with more canvases than space to put them, the hallway is a made-to-order gallery.

Hallways are condemned to be bland only if you so choose. As the transition space from one wing of the home to another, a hallway should provide visual continuity between spaces. Decorating these passageways with collections is one way to ensure continuity and provide a finished look to the home.

Staircase Walls

Akin to the oft-overlooked hallway is the wall space abutting a staircase. This area often receives slightly more decorative treatment than the hall, but the effort frequently doesn't extend much beyond wallpaper or paint, perhaps wainscoting, and a couple of accessories such as mirrors or sconces.

Like the hallway, though, this staircase presents an opportunity for creativity with collections. Collections of ephemera such as cigar-box labels may find a welcome home here. Fancy handkerchiefs that have been stored in a cedar chest can be ironed, framed, and displayed to charming effect.

One of the most overlooked areas of the home for design treatment is the long, narrow hallway—yet this space affords an almost gallery-like backdrop for a wall-mounted collection.

If an obvious collection for this space doesn't already exist, take inventory of your household. Chances are, there is something in your home—maybe hats, old illustrated sheet music, or quaint watercolor postcards that you've forgotten about—that could be retrieved as a design element to enliven the walls of the staircase.

Rec Rooms

For no good reason, homeowners are often resigned to having the recreation room (generally found in the basement) as nothing more than a repository for junk. This room, understandably, may not be the best place for the home's most stellar design statement, but in a well-designed home, it's inexcusable to cut off all creativity as soon as you descend the stairs.

Rec rooms are meant to be invitations to fun, not only in how they are used but also in how they are decorated. Less formal than other central living spaces, they can be more intimate, disclosing a little more personal or family history.

Found objects from vacations spent hiking or beachcombing can be organized and displayed: sinewy driftwood from Oregon piled in an oversized primitive wooden bowl; speckled cobblestones pilfered from the coast of Maine and arranged along bookshelves; garnets from the Adirondacks and amethysts from Nova Scotia each filling an antique basket. These objects have amazing visual impact, lending a unique feeling of character to the room and imbuing it with a more organic, less plastic feel that's appropriate for how the room functions. These collectibles, as reminders of experiences and good times, make a house feel like a home.

Sometimes the rec room is primarily used by children—an easy excuse for parents to ignore its decorating potential. If this is where children spend a large percentage of their time, however, there is all the more reason to make sure the room is as visually stimulating as possible. Try not to confuse decorating the room with tidying up—the constant battle to hide all the toys and games in trunks and closets, or behind cabinet doors. Instead, redefine the term. Turn decorating into a vehicle for revealing the room's true character; bring out the toys, rather than concealing them.

Children's toys have such interesting shapes and fun primary colors it's surprising adults don't use them as collections to spice up other parts of the house. Staple American toys such as wooden blocks, Legos, Lincoln Logs, and Tinker Toys can all be organized on designated shelves or in straw laundry hampers as low-maintenance, functional collections. Aside from keeping like objects grouped together, no special arranging is necessary. Half the fun is created by the sight of a jumble of brightly colored objects heaped together by children's hands, without any formal adult efforts at composition.

Junk Rooms

Every collector's home has one—and so do those of many non-collectors. The junk room is where homeowners consign their overflow—boxes of holiday decorations, collections temporarily out of service, sports equipment, old paperbacks. Seldom is the room occupied by real junk. It's only the arrangement—or lack of it—that makes the room appear junky.

Instead of eyesores, junk rooms can be transformed into events almost painlessly, because all of the players are already in place. Take old golf clubs, tees, balls, and anything else associated with the game (like all those kitschy gag gifts for duffers that friends and family have given you over the years) out from their hiding places behind other "junk" in the room and exert a little creativity. Soon you'll have a witty display of collectibles your friends can walk past without the blindfold.

Pin small pegs or large nails into the wall in the shape of an inverted triangle and hang holiday ornaments on this newly fashioned Christmas tree that can stay up all year long. Not only have you injected a delightful sight into your junk room, you've hit on a practical solution to breakage and accessibility and cleared the floor of a few more boxes.

Above: Junk rooms or workshops can be pulled together for a finished look by adding appropriate collectibles such as these old shoemaker's cramps.

Opposite page: A cluster of old oil cans interspersed with vintage model cars makes an attractive still life.

Equestrians always have more tack than can be squeezed into the lockers of a stable tack room, and inevitably this surplus winds up in the junk room. Create a mini–tack room with your paraphernalia and call it an equestrian collection—for that's exactly what it is.

Sawhorses are easily made for saddles, and wall brackets allow halters, lead ropes, and bridles to be properly hung, tangle-free. Lunge whips, riding crops, and derbies make an interesting still life, augmented by framed photographs of your horse or horses, ribbons, winning show numbers, and any other memorabilia you or your children have accrued. Saddle blankets add color to the wall or the floor. An old stall sign bearing your horse's name and hung on the wall serves as a title for your collection.

A cast-off child's bookshelf or even a group of old boards painted or stained and supported by brackets allows quick retrieval of favorite volumes of paperbacks stored in the junk room. Why take up floor space with unsightly cardboard boxes when the books can be more efficiently contained in a display that's both visual and functional?

Garage

Antique tools, farm implements, and old oil cans don't fit into the design of every room, but are great collectibles, nonetheless. There is no rule that excludes the garage from containing provocative displays of collectibles—or from being an area worthy of good design. Rustic wooden workbenches are naturals for displaying such collections, as is any existing shelving, although the latter probably lacks the character of the old furnishings.

Regional outdoor collectibles make the garage a favorite conversation item in its own right. In the American West and Southwest, where barbed wire is prevalent, this collectible finds a beckoning home on the not-too-fancy walls of the garage. Here, the various types of barbed wire (and there are many—entire books have been written cataloging the subject) can be displayed in field-guide fashion, one below the other.

In Maine or in Canada's Maritimes, it may be a collection of lobster traps and painted wooden lobster buoys that warms up the perimeters of the garage. Old garden tools supported on the wall by nothing more sophisticated than nails are appropriate collections for any region. Watering cans arranged on the floor, a shelf, or a workbench add interest. The most obvious candidates for the garage—mounted collections of license plates, hubcaps, sports-car prints, and racing photographs—shouldn't be forgotten simply because they are familiar.

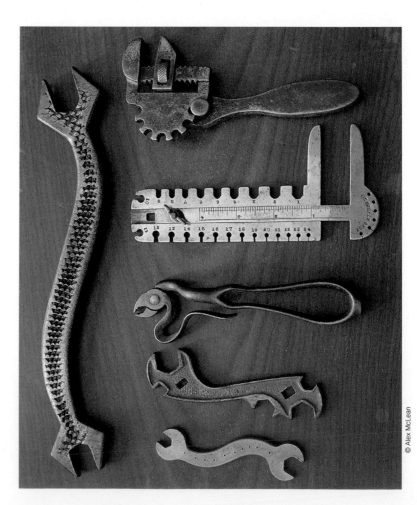

Right: Old tools, many hand-forged, have a rich history that lends character to any room. *Opposite page:* A brick wall in an old garage gains unexpected verve as the background for a collection of large neon advertising signs.

Linen Closets

Probably the most unlikely of all spaces in the home to be considered for displaying a collection is the linen closet. About as far as most people get in their association of closets with collections is as storage space. Yet here is an area already equipped with shelves, tucked discreetly behind a door, awaiting a viewing only when it's convenient. The closet invites a collection that you don't want vying for attention all of the time, or that simply doesn't conform to the remainder of the home's decor.

A designer told me how a friend of his turned to the linen closet as the answer to what to do with her collection of Christmas villages. The whimsical villages were too wonderful to pack away in boxes, out of sight for most of the year, but as a seasonal collection, they also understandably weren't considered appropriate by the owner as a permanent fixture in her home's interior design. The linen closet was the perfect solution. The collection could be on permanent display here for the owner's enjoyment—and that of any of her friends who might be interested. She went to great care making sure the pieces were properly displayed, even to the point of having special lighting installed. Best of all, though, the wonderful display was a hidden treasure, minding its own seasonal business without creating confusion for the other parts of the home.

Guest Rooms

If your own home doesn't have one, a friend's undoubtedly does: a guest room clothed entirely in plain white walls and second-rate furniture, which sticks out like the proverbial sore thumb from the rest of the house because of its conspicuous lack of design. The good news is it doesn't have to be that way.

Investigate some of your children's (or your own) old artwork, toys, dolls, and stuffed animals stored in the attic. A quick browse will turn up enough fun items to comprise a collection that will put some snap into the bland guest room. Old books and photos might also find a happier home in the guest room than stuffed away in boxes.

The guest room can also present an opportunity for decorating with collections that you might not want in the main rooms of your home. If you have a collection that just doesn't seem to belong, try it in the guest room. Or, if the room is to receive cast-off furnishings, why not make them ones that smack of style? Fifties furnishings are among the hottest collectibles going. Instead of the twenty-year-old, finished-yourself chest, dresser, and nightstand currently in the room, bring in 1950s pieces and make a statement. An entire room done in a collection of 1950s furniture and accessories is guaranteed to be one of the more interesting rooms in the house.

Opposite page: Diverse collections of Victoriana have been carefully placed to give this guest bedroom a distinctive elegance.

Dressing Areas

For an article I wrote about seven years ago, I encountered a part of a home so surprisingly well designed that it has stuck in my memory ever since. The home actually was the pint-size condo of Houston designer Carol Zimmerman, and the feature of it that I remember best was the dressing area. Because of limited space, Carol didn't have the luxury of using a lot of superfluous design elements on the walls or as furnishings. Every available surface was needed for utilitarian purposes, to hold her clothing and jewelry. But as a designer, and a person with incredible personal style, Carol demanded that every portion of her home be expressive.

Her solution was to make the most of what she had. She ornamented the walls with her collections of ethnic jewelry—a decision that saved space while bringing vivid color and interest to what would otherwise have been an ignored area. She removed the doors from her closet and arranged the contents in yet more vibrant displays of collections—a top shelf just for funky hats, another shelf for what can only be described as art shoes. Hanging clothes were organized so that even these had smashing visual impact.

The moral of this tale is, look at your dressing area with a fresh eye. Can you turn chaos into character?

You may be able to hang belts, scarves, handbags, and other accessories from the walls, providing accessible yet decorative storage. Pile colorful sweaters on open shelves or fill a basket with socks. A little imagination can make a crowded dressing room into an organized collection.

Right: Why hide away exotic earrings and necklaces in a jewelry box or drawer, when they make an art statement in their own right? Displayed directly on the wall, these three-dimensional collectibles possess power in number and can be appreciated all of the time, instead of only when worn. *Opposite page:* This walk-in closet has been customized to house a valuable collection of vintage costume jewelry.

Bathrooms

Earlier I mentioned a Dallas designer, Beverly Fields, who collects contemporary art and whose son is an artist. When I visited Beverly's home, it was a cornucopia of canvases that overflowed right into the bathroom. What a treat to be freshening up in front of Beverly's bathroom mirror, surrounded by a museumful of great contemporary art in this unlikeliest of settings.

Fine art isn't mandatory for designing a bathroom with collections, however. The most mundane items stored in drawers and cabinets can be arranged as collections in baskets, on shelves, on the vanity or dressing table, or on the wall. In the homes of friends who have no background in design, I've experienced real pleasure gazing at inventive displays of headbands and barrettes hanging from hooks; a whole collection of feather jewelry suspended from simple pegboards on the wall; stacks of early twentieth-century periodicals with their marvelous cover illustrations gathered in magazine racks; baskets of sweet-smelling, prettily wrapped soaps; old shaving mugs, brushes, and razors from grandfathers and great-grandfathers, presented alongside a slick European sink.

Forgotten Faces

Just as some rooms are forgotten as potential display spaces, so are certain furnishings and areas within a room. The more unlikely the furnishing or location, however, the more intriguing it will be. It is the unanticipated—the juxtaposition of disparate elements—that most invigorates an interior design.

© Peter Paige

Underfoot

Whatever the room, one important but frequently over-looked area also deserves attention: the floor. Look straight to the floor for placing a grouping of old leather luggage—no tabletop or trunk is necessary. A collection of antique or primitive drums also forms a beautiful arrangement when placed directly on the floor. The variation in height offered by a low-to-the-ground collection forces the viewer to shift down from eye-level focal points and get out of the rut of a single vantage point. What this means for the design of the room as a whole is a new level of depth and character.

Look not only to the surfaces of tables for potential collecting space but to the negative space beneath them, on the floor. The small circumference beneath a tiny tripod table may be just the place for placing an old wooden bowl filled with miniature leather-bound classics or a collection of folk-art crucifixes displayed upright on a wooden board outfitted with nail-head supports for each cross.

The floor is the answer to collections you want on view but fear might damage the finishes of your furniture. Jagged quartz crystals—natural beauty at its best—are sure to scratch a finely polished finish. The floor space beneath a piece of furniture is safe for them, however, and is still a defined area, its perimeters delineated by the furnishing above.

Opposite page: A bathroom shelf serves as a neutral backdrop for a collection of leaded glass perfume bottles, bringing elegance to a usually plain space. ***Above, left:*** Both indoor and outdoor walking surfaces, whether they are hardwood floors or brick patios, deserve attention as possible design focal points via collectibles. A collection of terra-cotta urns imbues this outdoor space with Southwestern character. ***Left:*** Colorfully painted birdhouses bring this corner to life.

© Nancy Hill/Courtesy House Beatiful's Home Remodeling & Decorating

EXPLORE THE UNEXPECTED

DESIGNING WITH COLLECTIBLES

© Wayne Ruple/Photri

Climb the Stairs

You climb the stairs every day. Why not have a collection of shoes climb them every day, all day long? Unless they're extremely narrow, stairs are another surface practically begging for design attention. Antique iron doorstops plopped one to a stair also make the trudge up and down less tiresome. These folksy collectibles are obviously harmonious with antique architecture, but for even more splash, why not display them or a similar vintage collection up the metal stairs of a minimalistic contemporary home? The tension between primitive and high-tech is packed with power.

Windowsills

Furnishings aren't the exclusive licensees of collectibles in home design. As kids, we were all aware of the value of the windowsill as a platform for our favorite figurines. For some reason, as adults we've lost sight of this practical design trick, perhaps due to a false sense of sophistication. (Or, maybe, we were repulsed after seeing too many unfortunate displays of ugly kitsch in windows!)

Especially for small collectibles, however, the windowsill is an excellent display area. In a traditional home, inkwells arranged along one windowsill of a room create an elegant vignette that encourages the eye to encompass all of the room.

In a country home with a blue-and-white color scheme, a collection of cobalt bottles—even fifty-cent flea market finds like the old Phillips Milk of Magnesia bottles—at the window creates some ethereal effects in natural light.

In the Manhattan brownstone of the late Dr. Robert Bishop, who was director of the Museum of American Folk Art, the living room windowsills were capacious. Bob, a consummate collector of every kind of folk art, used the space to display museum-quality folk-art carvings of everything from owls to Adam and Eve. Who says windowsill collections have to be kitsch?

Opposite page: The steps of a staircase are for more than walking. This collection of stoneware jugs and folk art watermelons climbs the stairs of a farmhouse with lighthearted warmth. ***Above:*** Simple narrow boards transform a plain window into an excellent showcase for a collection of old bottles, which benefit from the light shining through them.

Beams and Boards

Sometimes the architectural elements of a home—its structural members—are display surfaces awaiting a collection. Such was the case in the restored pre–Civil War barn used as a studio for North Carolina artist Bob Timberlake. In the upstairs quarters where he paints, Bob found the perfect place to display his collection of miniature canoes—along one of the old barn support beams where the wall meets the ceiling. He simply hammered a few nails into the beam and propped up the canoes. Putting this structural element to such atypical service resulted in a riveting exhibition of a favorite collection.

Look Up

Using overhead beams as containers for collections is no secret to country homeowners, who festoon the architectural elements in their houses with collections of baskets, antique cookware, beeswax candles, and herbs. Saddlebags and American Indian medicine bags are among other collectibles that can be effectively displayed in this manner. Try hanging mobiles, kites, and model airplanes from a lofty perch and letting the eye soar.

Balconies

Many upstairs spaces include balconies as part of the architecture. Spread a collection of wool Pendleton or Beacon camp blankets, with their warm lodge colors, across the railing for a vivid splash of color that can be appreciated from both upstairs and down. Drape quilts or other interesting fabrics the same way for an unexpected surprise.

Walls

Walls aren't limited to collections of art canvases. Enormous possibilities exist here for displaying all kinds of collectibles that can be framed or in some way affixed directly to the wall.

At the Kedron Valley Inn in South Woodstock, Vermont, owner Merrily Comins inherited a trunk of quilts that had been in her family for generations. Many were in perfect condition, with exquisite designs, colors, and craftsmanship, and went straight to the walls as focal points for various rooms in the inn. Others, however, hadn't fared so well over the years. Rather than part with these deteriorating quilts, Merrily cut them into pieces, salvaging the best sections as painting-size squares and rectangles she then had framed and mounted like any other wall art. The small quilt pieces have the appeal of paintings and certainly garner more attention from this display than they would have received in the storage pile.

Pegboard

Parental admonishments to the children at the dinner table to keep their chairs flat on the floor hold little sway when the chairs under discussion comprise a collection. Instead of being planted on the floor, a collection of chairs can be given a dynamite presentation thanks to pegboard, which allows them to be hung from the walls.

The Shakers always hung their lightweight, ladder-back chairs from pegboard for a practical reason: to keep them off the floor to free up space for walking and working. They turned the chairs upside down to prevent dust from settling on the side that would be sat upon.

These days not too many people care about whether or not a little dust settles on a chair seat. They emulate the Shakers' pegboard treatment of chairs for a different reason: because it looks good. The chairs needn't be authentic Shaker for this look to work. All that's necessary is that the chairs be light enough to hang without pulling the pegboard out from the wall. Because of their smaller scale and, thus, lighter weight, children's chairs are especially popular choices for a pegboard treatment.

Other, smaller collectibles become more noticeable when exhibited from pegboard. In my own home, pegboard was the solution for one of my favorite collections: 1920s-era (and earlier) beaded bags, some of which had belonged to my grandmother and great-grandmother, others that I had acquired on travels, and still more that had been given to me as gifts. Despite my special feeling for these pieces, until I opted for pegboard, I really had nowhere to display them (except for a few of the family bags, which I had had framed together). Now, all the bags hang happily in one place.

© José Luis Banus-March/FPG International

Opposite page: A balcony affords an ideal opportunity to display a collection, while at the same time drawing the eye upward to encompass more of the room's design. Custom shelves on this loft's upper level serve the same purpose. *Above:* The windowed balcony draws attention up to the collection of large urns.

New handbags also acquire the look of a collection when mounted from pegboard, and you can also show off a group of Bakelite bags—a collectible still going strong in popularity. Belts, jewelry, and canes also gain presence when shown from pegboard.

Eggs in a Basket

Archaeological excavations prove that decorative eggs have been a favorite collectible around the world since prehistoric times. Available today in every medium imaginable—glass, clay, bone, wood, precious metal and jewels, as well as painted, appliqued, or batiked—the eggs are usually displayed in individual egg holders. For fun, try putting them all in one basket. Or fill an ordinary egg carton from the grocery store with a collection of one genre, such as beautiful folk-art pysanky, the intricate, geometrically designed Ukrainians wax-resist eggs.

Printers' Drawers

Old wooden printers' drawers, once used to hold individual pieces of type, make excellent receptacles for all sorts of small collectibles. A single collection of numerous small pieces, such as wooden or glass miniature animals, makes an eye-catching display arranged in a printer's drawer—or go for a more eclectic look with a mix of items, such as coins, dice, buttons, or even seashells. Placed on the floor against a wall or hung up, printers' drawers filled with small treasures make an endlessly interesting display.

Above: Decorative eggs have been collected since prehistoric times, as documented by excavations. They can add an elegant ambiance to a space when displayed on formal stands, or they can create country warmth when simply plopped in a wicker basket. *Opposite page, above:* Heavy metal irons are naturals on cast-iron woodburning stoves, or even on an ironing board in the laundry room. *Opposite page, below and far left:* Printer's drawers have long been appreciated as display cases for miniature collectibles.

Hall Trees, Hat Racks

A hall tree or hat rack can be used as more than a place to toss your coat, hat, and scarf. It can be a choice spot for a collection of special hats, vests, bandanas, or canes. To create more interest, try placing the coatrack in an interior part of the home—in the living room, for example, far removed from its customary place beside an outside door.

Ladders

Everyone knows ladders are for reaching heights, not for furnishing a home, and it is precisely this understanding that makes a breach of the rule exciting. An old wooden ladder turned on the diagonal in a corner of a room is an unusual display surface for collectibles. Perch your collection of duck or fish decoys on its rungs—or hang old cup towels from them.

Ironing Boards

Ironing boards don't have to be relegated to a workroom. Pulled into a living space, an old wooden ironing board jolts, and thus commands attention. Its long, rectilinear shape is an ideal host for a collection—and an unusual one, in that it can float toward the center of a room, instead of being rigidly lined up along the wall, as is the case with most shelf surfaces.

Mannequins

To add a funky element to your decor, consider using an old department-store mannequin or dressmaker's form to display your collectibles. Drape scarves or shawls over the figure to create a quirky, unpretentious status. Watches, bracelets, and rings are perfect adornments for a mannequin hand or arm, and vintage clothing can be displayed to great advantage this way. You may even end up collecting the mannequins themselves, whose forms reflect the era in which they were made.

Above: In front of their collection of old photo buttons, these collectors have placed a model hand, which shows off a group of Bakelite and celluloid rings dating from 1920 to 1950. *Opposite page:* A group of lovable rag dolls finds a comfortable home in this large basket.

Old Shipping Crates

Old commercial wooden shipping crates come in many sizes and shapes and bear the names of all kinds of products and manufacturers. Interesting, inexpensive collectibles in their own right, they also make good receptacles for other, smaller collections. Stash a collection of antique wooden weights or bowling pins or balls in them, or a collection of children's sculpture (all those clay figures of hard-to-identify animals you dearly love), wooden flutes, or found objects.

If space is at a premium, select a good-size crate as a coffee table. Fill it with the desired collection, then top it with a slab of amber-tinted glass to size, with a few inches' overlap on all sides. Then sit back, prop your feet up, and enjoy this especially functional solution.

Old wooden manufacturers' boxes and shipping crates stamped with advertisements work wonders to embellish a corner.

Lobster Traps and Chicken Coops

Like shipping crates, these affordable conversation pieces can do double, even triple, duty serving as collectibles, containers for collections, and functional furnishings all at the same time. Flanking a chair or sofa, they make handy, low tables for resting a coffee cup or ashtray. Because of their rusticity, they are naturals for a country decor. But don't overlook incorporating them into a contemporary setting: Their interesting textures and offbeat flavor may be just the touch needed to warm a cool contemporary room. Store usable collections within them: a mound of kids' blocks or small quilted pillows that don't really work out on the sofa.

Benches and Church Pews

A primitive painted workbench, garden bench, or old church pew is a felicitous addition to a country, contemporary, or eclectic room. Chances are you won't really use the piece as seating; it's the visual function you value. It's only logical, then, that you put the furniture to some utilitarian service, and housing a collection is as good a way as any.

For the church pew, maybe it's a related collection you want to display: heirloom christening gowns, the Bible Grandmother carried in her wedding, collection plates from a church important in your family's history, your old catechism books, a collection of *santos* (Hispanic folk-art carvings of saints), or rosaries. The mix of textures and shapes permits a creative display.

The rustic bench lends itself to an easy-to-assemble arrangement of art books to which you want to give special, individual attention—something that's impossible to do in a coffee-table stack. Simply spread the books along the bench, one after the other, opening one to a favorite painting to break the monotony. Stand another upright to break the flat, linear pattern and catch the eye. Any country collection comprised of pieces of an appropriate size and scale for the bench can be displayed atop it: a collection of Shaker or Appalachian baskets; folk-art houses; or even dinged watering cans, intermixed with a couple of flowering houseplants in terra-cotta pots.

Left: Instead of scattering collections throughout a room or several rooms, try concentrating them in a single corner—but be careful to leave "air" in other parts of the space.

Sewing Machines

More than a decade ago, a new breed of restaurateurs—mainly ex-hippies turned entrepreneurs—decided on a design philosophy of "the funkier the better" for their brown-rice-and-smoothies establishments. In a feat of creative recycling, some inventive souls put old foot-pedal Singer sewing machines to adaptive reuse as intimate dining tables for two. Homeowners caught on, using the old family pieces in their houses as growing space for Boston ferns and other plants.

A more natural function for the vintage machines is obvious: as display areas for collections of antique sewing tools. Old spools, knitting needles, crochet hooks, sewing kits, button hooks, yarn balls, sewing baskets—even scraps of vintage fabric—rest in peace in these hospitable environs.

Pedestals

The pedestal's most common function is to display a single piece of sculpture. But when proportions are right, a small collection also can be given this highly visible presentation. The simplest, most inexpensive pieces—three urn-shaped vases in staggering heights made by three different contemporary potters—command the same attention as sculpture from their perch atop a pedestal.

Clothing for Collections

Antique brooches generally either get confined to the jewelry box or stashed beneath glass in an old store case that's then set atop a table or on a shelf. A more original presentation is achieved by pinning the brooches to a piece of vintage clothing, then displaying the clothing and collection with a coat hanger hung from the knob of an armoire or even from the top of a closet.

Likewise, a vest or scarf loaded with old political pins and suspended from a hanger or hook is more engaging than a collection of the pins laid flat on their backs.

Opposite page: Hung directly on the wall, a Victorian dress collection evokes nostalgia and romance in a bedroom.

All in the Family

Just as some rooms and potential display surfaces may go unnoticed in the design of a home, so do potential collections amid the familiar, everyday contents of a household. To add punch to your design at no expense, turn to some of the budding collections already at your fingertips: children's art, platform shoes from the 1970s, hot pants from the 1960s, love beads, concho belts, colorful bandannas, outmoded extra-wide men's ties, high school or college memorabilia. From the bundles and bags awaiting donation to a charitable organization, you can rediscover your personal history—the stuff of some of the most meaningful, droll, and in their own oddball way, sophisticated, of all possible collections. Collections don't have to be Blue Willow to be part of your decor.

Talking Heads

Visiting the Fenton, Michigan, home of folk artists Bill and Marcia Finks in the dead of winter was worth the chilly price. The Finks' home is a study in contrasts. In the dining room, classic nineteenth-century folk portraits in fine, lighted frames were joined by other representations of the human form: molded heads of Styrofoam and plastic with macabre, painted-on features. Marcia had casually stumbled across the pieces one day and asked if they were for sale. I think I can at least, in part, attribute my deepening friendship with Marcia to those delicious, witty heads. Who wouldn't be drawn to the person who first saw their potential?

Besides serving as collectibles in their own right, mannequins and mannequin heads are great spaces for displaying fashion collections: hats, jewelry, clothing. The best part is that these "people" don't have to be paradigms of good taste. Indeed, they shouldn't be. Load them down with belts and beads you wouldn't be caught dead wearing. As alter egos, they can act out for you. With a mannequin, the kitschier the better. This is pure fun, not brain surgery.

CHAPTER SEVEN

IN THE LIGHT

A common mistake in decorating is to ignore lighting altogether or to give it consideration only as an afterthought. The truth is, lighting is an essential part of good design and must be addressed at the same time the other major design decisions are being made.

Lighting can require construction alterations of its own. When undertaking a construction project such as the creation of niches or custom shelving for collectibles, lighting for the new areas should be wired and installed during the construction process, not afterward. How collections are to be lit can even determine whether a prospective furnishing for housing a collection should be purchased. All this underscores one point: Lighting must be addressed early on in the design process, to eliminate backtracking and deconstruction.

When designing with collections, it's important that special care be taken to bring exactly the right light source or sources to the pieces. Because attention in the room will be focused on the collection, the way in which it is lit must be planned in consideration of the overall lighting scheme of the room. For an interesting room, a variety of levels of lighting is necessary—general light to see by, accent light on key collectibles, pools of light on furnishings or walls (especially those containing collections), and, interspersed, pinpoints of light precisely touching a few special pieces of interest. To successfully light a collection, then, there must be an understanding of how the remainder of the room will be lit. This means that the process of planning lighting for a collection can't be isolated; it must be an integral part of the whole design process.

Right: The narrow spaces above this bookcase, flooded with light from a skylight, provide a crisp gallery setting for a framed collection of antique prints.

Downlights

Downlights can be installed in the ceiling wherever the room is wired for standard, overhead chandelier–type lighting. In a traditional room, using a chandelier may be the homeowner's preference. If so, try to take advantage of the light to call attention to collectibles. In a traditional living room, try placing a table of some sort beneath the fixture so that collections displayed on the tabletop can be drenched in this primary light source. If the chandelier is located above the dining room table, be sure some of your favorite collections are directly beneath it, waiting to soak up the light and bask in the attention.

For a more contemporary effect that works well in all styles of decor, not just contemporary, substitute subtle painted-metal downlights for the expected chandelier fixture. Instead of a single hanging fixture, several downlights can be strategically placed around a room for a greater dispersement of light. The more the light sources, the more interesting the room. Downlights can use either spotlight or floodlight bulbs. The effects of the two bulbs are different, so decide what you want to achieve before making a selection. Spotlights provide a beam of intense light and should be used only for bathing a relatively small targeted area of collectibles. Floodlights illuminate a larger space and can be used successfully to throw general light on larger case goods or wall shelving in which collections are spread out rather than highly concentrated.

Be sure that your downlights are actually aimed on your collections, not shining directly into the eyes of all who enter the room. The lighting can't be effective if it's blinding. Fortunately, some downlights swivel, allowing a precise aim.

A succession of downlights in a row is perfect for lighting an entryway or a room in which an entire wall features collections you want noticed. Many homes won't be wired for this kind of lighting, however, so some reconstruction may be in order.

One of the most beautiful effects of staggered downlights is to wash a wall in intermittent pools of light. It's the contrast between lighted and shaded spaces that creates exciting visual tension. Washing walls with a row of carefully situated downlights works in any room, even when the wall is completely bare, but it's especially successful when the wall holds a display of favorite collectibles.

Right: Track lighting is an inexpensive and highly flexible form of downlighting that can incorporate flood lights for illuminating a relatively large area and spotlights for highlighting a specific section of that area.

Track Lighting

A versatile use of downlights is possible with track lighting. Track lights are inexpensive and available everywhere, and they don't necessitate complex rewiring and reconstruction of the ceiling. When a room is already wired for conventional overhead lighting, metal tracks holding several individual lights can be mounted to the ceiling. The track can use both spotlights or floodlights, which can be pointed to illuminate any desired surface in the room. Any configuration of tracks is possible, too, such as a rectangle that extends around the perimeters of a room, or a horseshoe shape that travels around three walls.

Try mixing floodlights and spotlights on your track for a wonderful richness and depth of light. Illuminate an entire console or sideboard collection of china with a floodlight bulb, then shoot down a spotlight within that illuminated pool to single out the most important pieces of the collection.

Uplights

These canister lights come in all sizes and in both round and square shapes. As their name indicates, uplights point up, providing a light source from below. Frequently they are simply set directly onto the floor. Set beneath or to one side of a glass-topped table containing a collection of Lalique, uplights illuminate the crystal from the underside, creating wonderful striated effects that fully reveal the pieces' dazzling character and properties.

Uplights can be used as accent lighting for a small cluster of collectibles, such as a grouping of vases on a pedestal. On a glass shelving unit, consider uplights as at least a partial light source, especially when the collections on display also are transparent or translucent.

Because they are portable and sold everywhere and use a range of intensities of bulbs, uplights should be given serious consideration for use somewhere in the home that's designed with collections. Not only for the way in which they illuminate collections but also for the dramatic upward shadows they cast on a wall, uplights add an aura of intrigue and sophistication to the home.

When collectibles are presented in custom architectural cases, plan lighting prior to construction. The train set displayed here is lit very effectively from above.

© Balthazar Korab

© Balthazar Korab

© Jennifer Lévy

Above, left and right: Lighting can dramatically alter the mood of a collection. The custom case that holds this shell-and-flower still life offers two variations.

Left: Subtle lighting isn't always suitable for a collection, particularly if it is made up of numerous small items. In such a case, the entire collection in bold light is the most effective approach.

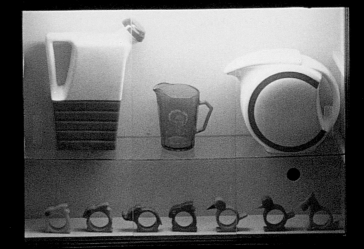

Pinpoint Spots

Especially important for collections displayed in entertainment centers or massive wall shelving are pinpoint spotlights. These tiny beams of light are accents that can be used wherever you want to call attention to an object. They can be located within shelving as an immediate, concentrated light source for the collectibles on display. Pinpoint spots should be used from the front to light opaque collectibles whose frontal exposure is what needs illuminating. For translucent or transparent collections such as amber glass, try back-lighting the pieces with pinpoints. Pinpoints can also be adhered directly to the wall and pointed in any direction to highlight an object of interest.

Just because you are focusing keenly on a collection with sharp but small pinpoints of light does not mean you should dismiss other types of lighting for the same collection. For the most interest, try several levels of light at one time: uplights to throw shadows on the furnishing that contains a collection, downlights with a floodlight bulb for an overall illumination of the furnishing, and tiny pinpoints from above, below, and in front or back of the individual collectibles.

Whenever you are displaying a collection in built-in architectural niches, each niche should be individually lighted with pinpoint spots. (If the light source isn't located in the niche itself, use downlights—even simple track lighting—to exactly highlight the architectural recess.)

Lamps

Lamps are probably the least interesting of all possible light sources in terms of quality of light. As a part of the room's furnishings, however, they can be among the most interesting pieces. And the simple fact is, for many interiors—especially those featuring traditional design, lamps remain a primary light source. Although lamplight can't compare

Architectural niches are only as successful as their lighting. The special bulbs within this niche bathe the collection in light, making it a focal point in the room.

with the dramatic, moody lighting achieved using a deft blend of uplights, downlights, spotlights, and pinpoints, they can at least be employed to illuminate collections so that the pieces are fully visible, if not greatly enhanced.

When other light sources besides conventional overhead chandeliers are not used in a room, be sure a lamp is located on the surface along with the display of collectibles, or at least nearby. Floor lamps—especially some of the wonderful, spare European styles with halogen lights—can be placed unobtrusively close to a collection and provide decent light without vying for attention with the collectibles.

In traditional rooms, where tables are the primary receptacles for collections, table lamps are essential for putting the objects in the light. Most opaque collections—especially those of clay or wood—can be adequately illuminated with simple lamplight. More shimmering surfaces—collections made of metal or glass—suffer when the only light source is a lamp (or, worse, the diffused light of a chandelier).

Bring in a Pro

The special effects that light can lend to a collection can't be overstated. Small fortunes can be invested for spectacular results, such as those attainable using laser lights. In addition to dramatizing collections, these sophisticated lighting systems, with their bold planes or shafts of light, can create architecture in a room.

Designing this kind of lighting, however, is generally beyond the capability of the layperson. Indeed, laser lighting is a highly specialized field of its own, beyond the grasp of most ASID designers. Licensed lighting specialists must be called in for the job, if this is the kind of lighting desired. If expense is not a concern, by all means don't hesitate to retain a qualified lighting designer. The difference the handiwork of this professional can make in creating a stage for beloved collections is that between night and day, dark and light.

A PRIMER ON DESIGNING WITH COLLECTIONS

DO: *Research your subject*

The best way to alleviate cold feet and avoid costly mistakes as a new collector is to first arm yourself with a thorough knowledge of your subject. Know your area of collecting inside and out. To acquire the necessary historical background and broad, overall knowledge of your collectible, read reference materials in the library. Stay current on prices and other changing variables in your field by reading periodicals. Start your own personal library of the best, most informative works on the topic.

DO: *Engage in hands-on study*

Augment the theoretical expertise gained from books and magazines with first-hand experience. Visit museums for a direct look at stellar examples of your chosen collectible. Attend auctions to hone your eye. Develop a rapport with local galleries or antiques dealers, who will allow you to touch, as well as look at, the collectible.

DO: *Go with your heart*

This applies not only to the area of collecting you select, but also to the specific pieces that will comprise that collection. Choose only collectibles that strongly appeal to your eye and your emotions.

DO: *Defy convention*

Nobody but you can decide what you like. Regardless of what may be currently popular on the collectible market, give yourself permission to ignore convention and buy whatever appeals to you, even though it may not be hot and trendy. Mass-market popularity is not an issue worth consideration. In the long run, pursuing an overlooked collectible may even bring a handsome payoff, should the market eventually catch up with your vision.

DO: *Consider your home decorating style*

Although collections need not always match the particular decorating style of a home, it is wise to consider how the objects will be integrated into the existing decor. Extremely fanciful, ornately decorative collections may work well in a Victorian home but will appear jarringly out of place in a primitive log cabin. On the other hand, a collection of stark contemporary sculpture may be just what is needed to give a nontraditional edge to a richly embellished Victorian home.

DON'T: *Equate collections with clutter*

Some would-be collectors may be scared away from the joyful experience of collecting by the false idea that collections connote clutter. This is especially true among admirers of contemporary design, who may find the notion of collections incompatible with their preferred style. In truth, every design style can be enhanced by collections. The judicious selection and tasteful display of collections safeguard against a cluttered look.

DON'T: *Be rigid*

Sometimes a strict adherence to certain principles of collecting—even such sensible rules as having fully researched your collectible area or acquiring a thorough knowledge of prices before buying—can mean lost opportunity. Try to stay flexible in your collecting. Weigh all the common-sense factors, but never forget to listen to your intuition and instinct—your heart.

DON'T: *Overlook the inexpensive*

Something that catches your eye as a possible collectible may bear a low pricetag that leads you to believe it is trivial and not worth collecting. If the object appeals to you, don't worry about whether it is "good" enough to merit collecting. Buy it and enjoy.

DO: *Pre-plan built-ins*

If your collection merits architectural changes in your home such as built-in shelving or niches or the adaptation of a closet, spend ample time planning. Determine the desired lighting before construction, so it can be properly and efficiently wired. Make sure you take into account not only the scale of existing pieces in the collection, but also allow some growing room for other pieces of various sizes you may acquire in the future.

DO: *Be selective about rooms*

Too many collectors take the easy way out, automatically assuming their collections should be housed in the most public, heavily trafficked room in the house. Although it is only natural to want a collection to receive optimum viewing, the most popular room is not always the best choice. Entry halls designed with collections can set a dynamic tone for the entire house in a way a living room, with all its other elements, cannot. Seek a happy marriage between the collections and their display rooms by matching personalities: a collection of watering cans is perfect for a solarium, old framed sheet music is ideal for a music room, antique inkwells belong in a study. After gaining some experience in design, you may wish to try a less likely match—but exercise care.

This colorful collection of fruit prints transforms an otherwise plain breakfast area into a cheery, welcoming space.

DON'T: *Impose artificial restrictions*

Insecurity limits creativity. Just because you own a Victorian home doesn't mean you must be restricted to decorating only with Victoriana. A contemporary art collection can be a striking counterpoint to the architecture. Don't hold any design dictates as absolutes. Make your own judgments, even when it means venturing out against the mainstream. This kind of risk produces the most original and vital interiors.

DON'T: *Show all or nothing*

Because you have paid good money for each piece in a collection doesn't require you to show all those pieces at the same time. As your collection grows, develop a habit of alternating the pieces that you display. This lends continual freshness to your home's decor.

DON'T: *Set limits*

As your collection of Staffordshire dogs accumulates and, along with it, your knowledge of the nineteenth-century Staffordshire pottery industry as a whole, you may want to buy some kind of Staffordshire other than dogs—Toby jugs, cats, or even spiel holders. Feel free. Exploring other avenues of collecting in no way dilutes your existing collection.

A collection of whimsical ceramic fruit brightens a kitchen shelf.

Above: Do mass small items—these colorful ceramic salt and pepper shakers have greater impact displayed in a group than if they are shown one set at a time.

Right: Don't ignore everyday items. This creative and quirky collection of toothpaste from around the world is eye-catching and fun. The ingenious method of hanging the tubers from binder clips shows a truly inventive mind.

DO: *Branch out*

Once you've gotten your feet wet as a collector, you may find your interests expanding or contracting—either way, this will require you to depart from your original plans. As your focus narrows or enlarges, feel free to follow that natural evolution of your interest. Collecting loses its appeal when it becomes limited or static.

DO: *Mass small objects*

For the most impact, gather a relatively large number of small collectibles together in a single display. The eye tends to ignore diminutive objects that are sparsely scattered. Visual power, in this case, results from number.

DO: *Balance*

Like a painting, a display of collectibles should be composed with balance. Balance is achieved by considering the size and shape of objects, and also their color, texture, and number. Balance colors and textures on both sides of an imaginary line bisecting the display. Finally, look at the display within the context of the room's balance.

DON'T: *Forget lighting*

Too often, the light shed upon a collection is an afterthought or not even a consideration at all. Lighting is an integral part of designing with collections. Make a point of lighting your collection to its best advantage.

DON'T: *Ignore everyday items*

Toys, sports gear, hats, costume jewelry—these items represent only a tiny portion of the vast array of potential collections already existing in most households. Don't ignore the possibilities these everyday items present. Take inventory of what's on hand and breathe new life into a neglected space with an eye-catching design with these pre-existing collectibles.

DON'T: *Dismiss the floor*

When searching for the right display surface, look to the floor. Baskets, boxes, books, and even paintings can add interest to a space without necessitating additional furniture, when positioned directly on the floor.

Opposite page: Don't forget to look outside the home for appropriate locations for housing a collection. Forgotten spaces such as walls of a shop or outbuilding, or the perimeters of a fence may be the right place—as this bunch of buoys demonstrates.

Even family photos can constitute a decorative collection, especially when displayed in beautiful frames.

DO: *Upgrade*

As your expertise or funds increase, improve the quality of your collection by upgrading. Sell or trade less valuable pieces for those of better quality, with no qualms of conscience. Of course, certain pieces—the first purchase in your collection or a gift from someone special—are always worth hanging onto, their value having little to do with quality or money.

DO: *Spread out*

As your collection grows, allow it to be displayed in more than one place. Try individual groupings in various parts of the same room, or create continuity throughout the home by spreading groups from room to room.

DO: *Mix sparingly*

When creating a mixed display of your collection with other accessories or objets d'art, display the collection with only a few other objects. This ensures that the items recognizably comprise a collection, and it eliminates the appearance of haphazardness and disorder. Other objects included in the display should relate in texture, color, size and design. If you are using more than one collection, select a limited number of items from each for showing at one time—an overly complicated mix detracts from the display's appeal.

DON'T: *Assume collections are money wasted*

Much of the fear of collecting can be alleviated by the realization that no collectible is money lost. Every piece has some monetary value that can be recovered. With this in mind, don't allow yourself to become paralyzed with fear, foregoing a desired purchase because the initial cost is intimidating.

DON'T: *Display unrelated items*

A sure way to diminish or destroy the impact and beauty of good collections is to display unrelated objects in the same grouping or within overly close range. Japanese urns or French porcelains have little in common with earthy, split-oak woven baskets, and would look odd placed in close proximity. To give each collection its due, allow some visual distancing.

DON'T: *Force large collections into one massive display*

As a collection grows, it is not always practical or aesthetically pleasing to display it in its entirety in a single grouping. Don't destroy a collection's integrity by attempting to cram all the pieces into a single space. Try breaking the collection up into groups, instead.

DO: *Gauge mood*

Collections change not only the appearance but also the mood of a living space. Determine the desired mood of a room—bold and lively, spare and understated, or cozy and welcoming, for example—then implement a design using compatible collections.

DO: *Estimate space*

As much as collecting may be dictated by the heart, it requires cooperation from the head to be successful. The practical issue of how much available space can be devoted to a collection must be considered. Antiques of mammoth scale are fine in a home with a proportionate amount of space, but they will quickly overwhelm and cramp a tiny apartment. A few large pieces of art may create an illusion of space in a small area, whereas a profuse number of miniatures might only underscore the room's diminutive size.

DO: *Buy the best*

Though there are exceptions, a good rule of thumb in collecting is: always buy the best you can afford. The outstanding piece may cost more than two inferior ones combined, but it represents the difference between excellence and mediocrity in your collection.

DON'T: *Go with what's hot*

Folk art birdhouses, quilts, Fiestaware—at one time each of these was ignored as a collectible. Now that these items are in vogue, early collectors who had the foresight and confidence to buy them despite lack of popularity find themselves with valuable collections worth far more than what they originally paid. Trust your instincts, regardless of what is happening on the market. And remember: What's trendy today won't stay that way long. That, by definition, is the nature of trends.

DON'T: *Hang on*

If you are branching out into other collecting fields or improving your collection, you need not retain all of your earlier collectibles; it may be best for you to sell or trade some of those pieces you already have. Don't feel obligated to hang onto a collection once it has outlived its purpose. Collections are intended to be sources of fun, not guilt.

DON'T: *Be obvious*

Curio cabinets are the most obvious display surfaces for collections, but not the best. Seek other, more creative solutions for showing off your wares.

Egg decorating is an art practised around the world. When set atop a mirrored table, these beautifully painted eggs are shown off to great advantage.

Vintage jewelry is safe from accidental breakage but still very much on view in this old store display case.

DO: *Be inventive*

Although the aforementioned display surfaces are the ones most frequently employed with good results, they are by no means the only options. The more unusual the display surface, the more eye-catching the collection. Enlist such unusual elements as old rustic garden benches, small church pews, or antique baby carriages for an unusual, exciting presentation.

DO: *Note forgotten spaces*

Hallways, guest rooms, bathrooms, basements, mudrooms, garages, laundry rooms, workshops, gardens, patios—all are spaces begging for design. Try your hand at decorating these forgotten places with collections—not necessarily your most valuable, but those that may prove to make a clever design statement.

DO: *Find the right container*

A wonderful collection that is creatively arranged in an artistic composition will lose its impact if it is shown on an inappropriate furnishing. Consider console tables, sideboards, entertainment centers, bookcases, custom shelving or niches, pedestals, windowsills, and mantels. Make sure the display unit you select blends with the style of your home.

DO: *Find the right angle*

Determine the best angle of presentation for the various components in your collection. Some will merit a side view, while others are best displayed from the front. Still others, such as ephemera, require viewing from above, so are best displayed flat on their backs, below eye level, for visibility. Another option for ephemera and some other types of collectibles such as fans or lace-edged handkerchiefs is to lay the pieces flat in a frame that is then hung on the wall.

DO: *Protect fragile pieces*

When the collectibles are fragile or susceptible to damage, be sure to select a display method that protects the pieces. Glass store cases, glass-covered frames or shadow boxes, or see-through containers—even those as unlikely as an old chicken coop or glass-topped wooden shipping crate—are among the possible selections.

Collections can announce the flavor and personality of a home even before the home has been entered, as illustrated by this collection of small wooden birdhouses displayed on the front porch.

Additional Photography Credits

FURTHER READING

Conway, Patricia, *Art for Everyday: The New Craft Movement*. New York: Clarkson N. Potter, Inc., 1990.

Gilliatt, Mary, *The Complete Book of Home Design*. New York: Little, Brown & Co., 1992.

Hilliard, Elizabeth, *Finishing Touches*. New York: Crown Publishers, Inc., 1990.

Klamkin, Marian, *Collectibles—A Compendium*. New York: Dolphin Books, Doubleday & Co., 1981.

Lindquist, David P., *The Official 1990 Identification and Price Guide to Antiques and Collectibles*. New York: The House of Collectibles, 1990.

Reno, Dawn, *The Official Identification and Price Guide to American Country Collectibles*. New York: The House of Collectibles, 1990.

Sloan, Susan P., ed., *Sloan's Guide to Antiques Dealers and Antiques-Related Services*. Boston: The Antique Press, 1992.

The Encyclopedia of Collectibles. Multiple vols., Time-Life Books.

Wissinger, Joanna. *Lost and Found: Decorating with Found Objects*. New York: MacMillan Publishers, 1991.

INDEX

A

Advertising pieces, *46, 78,* 93, *98, 99*
Americana, *37*
Arrangements
  small collectibles, *58, 59, 60, 84*
  still-life, 58, *65, 90, 123*
Art
  deco, *9,* 57
  fine, *21,* 95
  folk, 17, 20, 22, 42, 78, 107, 114, 135
  framed, *45*
  glass, *43,* 72
  prints, *120, 130*
Auctions, 30, 32

B

Bags, beaded, *56,* 109
Bakelite, 110, *112*
Balance
  asymmetric, 61
  in display, 61, 132
  symmetric, 61
Baseball memorabilia, *14*
Baskets, 57, 108, 110, *113,* 114
Bells, *33*
Bennington pottery, 80
Birdhouses, 80, *105,* 135, *137*
Black memorabilia, 14, 16, *16*
Books, 62, *74,* 85
Bottles, *45, 107*
  barber, *54*
Boxes, *18, 22,* 93, *93*
  lunch, *35*

manufacturer's, *114*
  shipping crates, 114, *114,* 136
Brushes, *29,* 104
Buttons, 110, *112*

C

Cabinets, 85
  closed, 71, 80, 82
  corner, 78, *79,* 80
  curio, 135
  glass-front, *61,* 80, 82
  open, 71
Candlesticks, 80, 85, *85*
Car models, *59,* 97
Catalogs, auction, 32
Chests, miniature, *79*
China, *83*
Clocks and watches, *65*
Clutter, 129
Coins, 110
Collecting
  associative, 14, 16–17
  available space for, 46, 48
  beginning, 27–35
  category decisions, 38–49
  compulsive, 87
  decorative, 18, 20
  decor blending, 42
  education in, 30, 32, 34
  feelings in, 12
  flexibility in, 129
  intrinsic, 12, 17
  investment, 20, 22
  mood in, 45, 123, 135
  quality in, 34
  rules, 27
  styles, 42

Collections. *See also* Memorabilia.
  advertising pieces, *46, 78,* 93, *98, 99*
  alternating, 72, 131
  Americana, *37*
  ancient artifacts, *21*
  art, *45*
  art deco, *9,* 57
  barbed wire, 57, 98
  barbershop items, 54, 104
  beaded bags, *56,* 109
  bells, *33*
  birdhouses, 80, *105,* 135, *137*
  books, 62, 74, 85
  bottles, 45, 107
  boxes, *18, 22,* 93, *93*
  brushes, *29,* 104
  buttons, 110, *112*
  candlesticks, 80, 85, *85*
  car models, *59*
  china, *83*
  cigar-box illustrations, 65
  clocks and watches, *65*
  coins, 110
  cookie jars, *32*
  country, *37*
  crystal, *23, 45*
  displaying, 53–67
  dolls, *38, 65, 113*
  eggs, 110, *110*
  ephemera, *39,* 65, 95
  fashion, 117
  Fiestaware, 29, *90,* 135
  figurines, *26,* 45
  folk art, 17, 20, 22, 42, 78, 107, 114, 135
  frames, *23*
  furniture, 62, 109
  glass, 57, 125
  art, *43,* 72
  globes, *67*
  Harlequin, *90*